JULIAN OF NORWICH

JULIAN OF NORWICH

Journeys into Joy

selected spiritual writings

introduced and edited by
John Nelson

New City Press
Hyde Park, New York

Published in the United States by New City Press
202 Cardinal Rd., Hyde Park, NY 12538
www.newcitypress.com
©2001 John Nelson

Cover picture: "Julian of Norwich." Used by permission of Lu Bro.
©1998 Lu Bro. Reproductions: Bridge Building Images, Inc., P.O. Box 1048
Burlington, VT 05402; www.BridgeBuilding.com.
Cover design by Nick Cianfarani

Library of Congress Cataloging-in-Publication Data:

Julian, of Norwich, b. 1343.
    Journeys into joy : selected spiritual writings / introduced and edited by John Nelson.
        p. cm.
    Includes bibliographical references.
    ISBN 1-56548-134-8
    1. Meditations. I. Nelson, John, 1931- II. Title.

BV4832.3 J85 2001
242--dc21   2001016268

All royalties from sales of this book are received directly by the Community of Poor Clares, Arundel,
West Sussex, England to support its life of apostolic prayer for the world, within the first Rule for
religious life written by a woman, St. Clare, to live according to the perfection of the Gospel—a
purpose also pursued by the first known woman writer of English prose, Mother Julian, in recording
her Revelation.

Printed in Canada

Contents

This is a Revelation of Love that Jesus Christ, our endless bliss, gave in sixteen visions. He revealed it all because he wants it to be better known than it is. And as we come to know it he will give us grace to love him and cling to him. In our creation we had a beginning, but the love in which he created us was in him for ever and never had a beginning: In this love we have our beginning. All this we shall see in God without end.

Mother Julian of Norwich
from the first and last words
of her manuscript
describing her visions
Revelations of Divine Love, ch. 1; ch. 86

Introduction

This is a Revelation of Love

The purpose of this book

Speaking to us across the six centuries which have passed since she put pen to paper, Julian of Norwich is very much a teacher, guide and friend for today, our own times. As good wine matures and ripens in the keeping, so also the years have seasoned the significance and relevance of Julian's optimistic and profound insights into the reality of our God of hope and love.

As we step out onto the journey which we each make through this life in returning to that from which we came, we are not alone. We travel with each other. We can also choose Julian as an invigorating companion and wise pathfinder. With concrete imagery and vivid language she shows us afresh the One who beckons us onward, who points our way, who traces out the steps by which we make the most expeditious and rewarding progress.

God is the divine Being from whom all human beings come and into whom all are called as one. Jesus prayed, "May they all be one. Father, may they be one in us" (Jn 17:21). We are called to oneness with the divine nature, in the many-splendored creativeness of the One who gifts and graces us as God's children. *God's gifted grace brings our lovely human nature back again to the place it started from — that is, in God — only with greater splendor and glory because grace works with such power for good,* as Julian comments in chapter 63 of *Revelations of Divine Love.*

Paul describes our unveiling, even in this life, by which we grow brighter and brighter as we are changed into the image which we now reflect (2 Cor 3:18). In our loving response to the call of Love, we are changed into an increasingly faithful image of God in Christ. He fires our understanding, directs our way, soothes our conscience, encourages our soul, and illumines our heart, Julian taught.[1] We become holy; that is, healed and made whole. The root of the word *holy* is in the words *hale* and *whole.* In heaven we shall be wholly complete, completely real. Creation is always journeying towards perfection.

We are in a process of change; we are on a journey. That is the purpose of this book — to follow Julian as she shows the path to healing and wholeness through her experience of the Revelation of love given to her by Jesus himself. In this progress we have the additional help of the light shed on our path by Scripture which is the Word of God, and by the insights and understandings of the Church, the Body of Christ.

It is a revelation of the cosmic completeness to which we are destined in our God, the One who is All. We go to him bearing our varied and manifold gifts of love, as the Magi bore to the manger their offerings of recognition, welcome and adoration.

---

1. Cf. RDL ch. 61.

What image of God do we hold?

The dilatory schoolboy unwillingly picking his way to school shows by his actions the sort of image he has of school, the end of his journey. We Christians also show what image we have of God as we wend our way through life. We show in our actions the effects of what we hold in our minds as our image of that to which we are called. We are called to rejoice in the Lord (cf. Phil 3:1) and to have such joy that there is no limit to our hope and expectations (Rom 15:13). We are called to be living Gospels, showing forth the good news to others that they may come to it and share it. But we can only give what we have gained. We cannot share what we do not have.

The Israelites in their great exodus from slavery in Egypt did not take a direct way to the promised land. They spent many years on a circuitous route during which they rebelled, even hankering for the pleasures and security of their former slavery in Egypt. In their waywardness they even made a false image, from the gold of this world, and called it God (Ex 32:1-5). Nevertheless, broken away from this self-willed childishness, in their onward desert journeying they slowly learned a daily dependence upon the true God. They were released from their false image.

This wayward journeying is surely often reflected in our own lives, in which we may carry with us a false image of God. We may have stayed, into adult life, with half-remembered childish ideas gained from early religious guidance. Or our image may have derived from a harsh and judgmental teaching based on misunderstanding of the Old Testament. Or we may have suffered human teaching and example which has lacked goodness or veracity and integrity. But perhaps we have simply rebelled and wanted to do things our way, and so have found excuse to do so. In that case, for we are all sinners, a false image is a handy thing to have, for we can always put the blame elsewhere. As Adam said by way of excuse, "It was not me, it was the woman." And Eve also passed the blame on, in her turn (Gn 3:12-13).

Our progress to our promised land has therefore to be prompted and renewed by God's revelations and visitations. We have to be stripped of our false assumptions and mis-understandings so that we may be clothed anew in the truth — the truth which we had already been given and, deep down, knew, but which we mired and failed to admire. For the testament of the Old Covenant also reveals the compre-hensive love of the Father God who is fatherly and motherly[2] and unendingly, patiently forgiving.[3] Judgment is of our own making; we draw it down on ourselves — How often have I longed to gather you as a mother hen gathers her chicks under her wings, and you refused (Mt 23:37), said Jesus, who came to us to teach us all over again that God is love, revealing his New Covenant with us in which those who do not judge will not be judged (Lk 6:37).

Called by name

In our journeys into joy in Julian's company, we can put aside any untrue images of God as the Israelites destroyed their ridiculous golden calf. We rediscover — or, if the reader

---

2. Julian's discussion of the motherly attributes of Christ should not be thought to have been a new insight, nor one which marks her out as being a proto-feminist. Julian at no time writes of this perception as being a new revelation nor does she treat it as exceptional. John Julian notes, "It is a venerable tradition supported by Adam of Perseigne, Aeldred, Albert the Great, Anselm, Aquinas, Augustine, Bernard of Cluny, Bonaventure, Bridget of Sweden, Catherine of Siena, Clement of Alexandria, Dante, William Flete, Gilbert of Hoyland, Guerric of Igny, Guigo II the Carthusian, Helinand of Froidmont, Isaas of Stella, Margery Kempe, Peter Lombard, Ludolph of Saxony, Marguerite of Oingt, Mechtild of Magdeburg, Richard Rolle, William of Saint Thierry, the *Ancrene Riwle,* the *Stimulus Amoris.*" (John Julian OJN, *A Lesson of Love,* Darton Longman & Todd, London, 1988). See also Is 66:13 and Mt 23:37.

3. For example Is 66:13; 54:4-8; 44:1-4; 43:1-5; 63:7-9; Eccl 2:3-11, etc.

is enquiringly coming to Jesus from unbelief, he or she will newly discover — our glorious God of infinite gentleness and passionate love who is so small that he lives and delights in each of our hearts, filling with glory our essential nature, our fundamental being. Our glorious God who is also so without limit, so powerfully great, and of such wondrous majesty that all creation cannot hold him, and is as nothing beside him. He is not just loving, he is love. He is not just joyful, he is joy. He is not just beautiful, he is beauty. He is not just good, he is goodness. All his manifold and amazing attributes are his very being, for he is I AM WHO AM (YAHWEH).

He has revealed his Name and his nature to us; to disclose one's name is to make oneself known to others; in a way to hand oneself over by becoming accessible, capable of being known more intimately and addressed personally.[4] He has called us by name to him (Is 43:1), for us to share his very nature (2 Pt 1:4) and become like him. Our destiny is to be one-ed with him (Jn 17:21), and so become our true selves, more realized than ever we could humanly dream or long for.

With Julian's teaching and encouragement, and in our renewed understanding and image of him, we can joyfully run like little children towards him and into his very arms; for Jesus himself, the Son of the Father, said we should welcome the kingdom of God like a little child (Lk 18:17). Then as a mother comforts a child, we shall be comforted (Is 66:13).

Julian's world

In Julian's times during the fourteenth century, religion was a lively, pervasive, daily affair. Life was, for most, short and hard. Eternity must have seemed so often only a hair's breadth away, for mankind's defences against disease and

---

4. CCC 203.

death were few and hardly effective. The outbreak of the Black Death plague in the middle years of the century had the effect of a major nuclear disaster. About one third of the population of Europe perished, while outbreaks of the plague continued to return periodically. Julian's own home town, Norwich, is thought to have had a population of some thirteen thousand in 1300. By 1373, the year her Revelation was shown to her, the town's population had been reduced to under six thousand. Meanwhile, men and money were sucked from the economy to sustain the English attempts from 1337, in the Hundred Years War, to gain French territory and to resurrect what had been the Anglo-Norman empire resulting from the Norman Conquest. The shortage of agricultural labor caused by the Black Death led the peasants to demand higher wages; the constant and arrogant collection of war-taxes angered the more well-to-do farmers and tradesmen. Social unrest and violent reprisals followed, and were most dramatically evidenced in the Peasants' Revolt of 1381.

To all this was added religious conflict, for John Wycliffe and his Lollard followers were spreading ideas which attacked the wealth and institutional power of the Church, seeking a return to a more primitive, simpler Christianity and the pre-eminence of a vernacular Bible. Only three years after Julian's Revelations were shown to her, Wycliffe's On Civil Dominion was published, proposing a propertyless Church. Julian's times were indeed those of great social turmoil, revolutionary danger, and religious questioning.

So it was clearly wise during the short span of this unsatisfactory earthly life to prepare for what in all likelihood would be faced so very soon. For what was to be one's fate after death — heavenly bliss among the saints or hellish damnation in undesirable company — was of eternal duration, while the time of preparation here was brief. The fear of Yahweh is a life-giving spring for eluding the snares of death

(Prv 14:27) would be a saying which would ring as very true in the ears of a person of those days. Religion was indeed a daily concern for the prudent.

Julian's Revelation

What could be more natural than that the image of Jesus crucified and suffering would speak so directly and relevantly to the popular mind in all these circumstances, for had he not in his death gone down to hell and rescued those imprisoned there who were to be saved (cf. Jn 5:25; Mt 12:40; Rom 10:7; Eph 4:9)? Had he not been poor with nowhere to lay his head (cf. Mt 8:20; Lk 9:58)? Had he not called all to his cross, that their yoke might be made easy (cf. Mt 16:24; 11:30; Mk 8:34; Lk 9:23)? Indeed, Julian opens her account of her visions by telling us that sometime prior to them she had asked three gifts from God: to have more mind of — that is, to truly understand — Jesus' Passion; to suffer sickness at the age of thirty in order to experience and be cleansed by God's mercy, that after she might live more to his glory; and to have the three wounds of true sorrow for sin, of kind natural compassion, and of deep longing for God.

It was the third Sunday after Easter, May 8, 1373. Julian's prayer to be seriously sick almost to the point of death had been answered. She had lain ill for a week, in pain, and now her body was paralyzed from the waist down. Her parish priest had been called in to be by her while she died. He had brought a crucifix to hold before her for her to gaze at it and be comforted. Her sight weakened and all became dark to her, except for the crucifix which remained mysteriously lit. The upper part of her body then began to die, she could feel little, and her breathing faltered. She was convinced her life had ended. It was early in the morning, about four o'clock. Suddenly, all pain left her and she became as well as she had ever been, though she was still not sure that she would live.

Equally suddenly, amid this change, she thought she should ask God for the fulfilment of her second request; to fully experience and to compassionately understand Christ's Passion. Immediately she "saw the red blood trickle down from under the garland of thorns . . . just as it was in the time of his Passion . . . it was none other than Jesus who showed this vision to me."

The first fifteen of the visions were shown to Julian over the course of five hours. They ceased at a time past nine o'clock that same morning. There followed a period of self-doubt by Julian amid a return of the illness. In this loss of faith in the visions, she lay still and trusted to God's mercy despite an interlude in which she saw, or dreamed that she saw, the devil assaulting her. Eventually she passed to great peace and rest, with quietness of conscience, and freedom from illness. That same evening of the seventh day the sixteenth vision was shown to her.

For some twenty years, in the early period of which she wrote her initial short account of the Revelation, Julian pondered its full implications. In about 1393 she concluded her long written account, from which the present selection of readings is compiled.

The teachings of the Revelation

Julian lived to a ripe old age. It seems that she attracted little attention beyond her own neighborhood. Her writings disappeared, only to emerge into full light again in the version edited by Grace Warrack and published in 1901. Since then, she has become recognized as the first woman writer of English prose, and a widely-read teacher of a very warm-hearted, loving and totally trusting approach to God which is absolutely compatible with, and complementary to, the insights of that other great teacher, and Doctor of the Church, Thérèse of Lisieux. Thérèse's writings were first published in

1898, within three years of the 1901 publication of Julian's work. Both books achieved wide sales and reached out to encourage, refresh and stimulate so many who immediately recognized their relevance to our lives in modern times.

Both women reveal a way for us of loving simplicity and confident trust within a revivified insight into the truth of an intimate and close God who longs and thirsts for us; a God who welcomes us as children into the arms of a parent. A God who is all. Both women show us a way to self-acceptance, integration and realization through our acceptance of all others in the unchanging and untiring acceptance everlastingly offered us by our Creator, who ever seeks us even when we never seek nor respond. Both women reveal to us a mendicant God; one who, in essence whole, impassible and without need, nevertheless in outreach allows the need for us to make almighty God a beggar for our love. Both women focus on the humanity of Jesus, the savior God clothed in human nature that we might become clothed in the nature of God. Both women show us the way of a child of God in the peace and joy which Jesus promised us and which a worldly, adult sophistication can never understand. We cannot rise higher than the state of graced, gifted childhood; for we can do nothing of ourselves alone. Jesus wants us to be like a little child who rushes quickly to its mother for help when hurt or frightened, wrote Julian.[5]

For it is the eyes of children, babes in arms, who see God; and the lips of children, babes in arms, who sing of God (Ps 8:2; Mt 21:16; cf. Mt 18:3).

That coincidence of teaching, publication, and popularity of Julian's and Thérèse's works is a most remarkable happening. Amid the modern world and its loss of faith, amid its obsession with the fruit of the tree of knowledge of good

---

5. RDL ch. 61.

and evil in its conviction that we can become gods (cf. Gn 3:1-5) without need of God, two weak, unknown, hidden women, in lives separated by five hundred years,[6] have spoken and have been heard because they speak truth and point the way to life and joy. Seemingly it was necessary that their understandings be the means of restoring and reminding us of a proper, truthful balance in our perception of God, the everlasting Father who is a tender, longing, motherly parent. Through them is once again revealed the perfect completeness of the Divinity, which we, in the equal dignity of our different genders, reflect. The feminine and masculine — that by which we are differentiated, and that of both which we each contain — need each other in fruitful partnership to be the means for God to reveal the wholeness of the truth. Julian commented: I saw every duty that God has given us toward fatherhood and motherhood is fulfilled in truly loving God.[7] In the freedom of this truth (Jn 8:32) we enter that joy which shall never be taken from us (Jn 16:22).

About the readings in this book

There are two important aspects of Julian's teaching which cannot be ignored without distorting her message. The first is

---

6. It is of interest to note that Julian's integrated insights and teaching were expressed in the twilight years of a feudal time in which women appear to have had greater social and spiritual status. In that earlier period girls became adult at twelve and boys at fourteen years. Women practiced medicine regularly during the thirteenth century; and the oldest text on education in France was by a woman. There followed a decline in that more balanced gender relationship during succeeding centuries, until the emergence of efforts toward gender equality as the twentieth century dawned — and coincidentally as Thérèse's and Julian's gentler insights and teachings both became known and influential. For an innovative study of the social and spiritual position of women in feudal and medieval times, see Régine Pernoud's *Women in the Days of the Cathedrals* (Ignatius Press, San Francisco, 1998).

7. RDL ch. 60.

that Julian roots her teaching in Scripture, it percolates her writing. She must have known the Bible well. This implies that she gained some knowledge of Latin during her protracted study of her Revelation, for she lived in days before the Church approved the translation of the Bible into the vernacular. Certainly, in her cell attached to Saint Julian's church (from which she gained the only name by which we know her, for we have no baptismal or family record of her) she would have had ready access to the Bible.

Therefore, each reading from Julian in this book is preceded by relevant Scripture. Her closeness to the Bible is demonstrated by the way in which these extracts have been so readily related to her writings. We can hardly go astray if we begin with the word of God, asking the Holy Spirit to open our eyes and heart to the truth in it.

The second aspect of Julian's writings is that she is founded on what she called "the everyday teaching of Holy Church." In any of her discussion of difficult points arising from her meditations on her Revelation, she specifically submits her will and judgement to that of the Church. Julian states that she believes all that Holy Church proposes and teaches. To wrest Julian's teaching from this context of Church would be to tear the heart out of her teaching, in which she urges that we should hold firmly to the faith of Holy Church and find in her our beloved mother who consoles us and helps us to understand, in union with all the saints.[8] She repeatedly refers to her "even-Christians," by which she means her fellow-members in the Church — and she knows that what she has seen and learned is intended for their assistance and encouragement as individuals and as a body.

Therefore, respecting this essential ecclesial dimension, and to enable Julian's teaching to be related to our contempo-

---

8. RDL ch. 61.

rary Church understandings of matters she discusses, the readings from the Revelations are followed by short extracts from the treasury of the universal Catechism of the Catholic Church. That Catechism is the latest and lasting fruit of the historic ecumenical Council of the Church held in the 1960's, called Vatican II, which opened the windows and doors of the Church onto the world, following the fortress years in the aftermath of the Reformation storms.

Daily portions

This volume is entitled *Journeys into Joy*. The word journey is derived from the French *jour*, day. A journey is a day's progress, a day's travel, a day's portion. Each tri-part reading, with its short, pointed prayer, can therefore be a journey, a day's portion. Each will render, under the guidance of the Holy Spirit, a fund of ideas and inspiration to enable the mind to remember and reflect on them during the rest of that day, whatever the day may otherwise contain in terms of work or leisure. The use of the readings is equally suitable for the individual and for groups engaged in prayer or study.

We are urged by Paul to pray without ceasing (1 Thes 5:17). This need not cause the reader any trepidation or perplexity. Augustine of Hippo said that our unceasing prayer is in our unceasing desire to be with God, to be accompanied by God. The continual love we then have for God is our constant prayer. It does not matter whether that desire to love is felt or is simply an intention held onto in arid dryness. We should never worry about feelings; they are not in our control to that extent. To try to pray is to pray. Then the heart is always open and longing. It is as simple as that.

With this in mind, it is hoped that the journeys in this book will provide a little daily fuel for the fire of love, whether it be bright with flames or damply smouldering. God just wants our "yes." He will do the rest, according to his wisdom.

Every one of us lives only to journey
further and further into the mountains.
No soul that seriously and constantly desires joy
will ever miss it.
Those who seek find.[9]

* * *

Abbreviations

RDL – Revelations of Divine Love
CCC – Catechism of the Catholic Church

NB: For simplicity and clarity, in the extracts from CCC all references to quotations from Church documents have been omitted and the quotation marks removed.

---

9. C.S. Lewis, *The Great Divorce*, Collins Fontana Books, London, 1972.

The First Revelation

Christ's Suffering for Love of Us

I saw the red blood trickle down from under the garland of thorns just as it was at the time of his Passion when the crown of thorns was pressed on his blessed head. And I saw very clearly and powerfully that Jesus, both God and Man who suffered thus for me, was the very same one who showed this vision to me without any intermediary.

And in that same vision, the Trinity suddenly filled my heart with the deepest joy. I immediately realised that this will be the permanent experience of those who go to heaven. For the Trinity is God: God is the Trinity. The Trinity is our maker, the Trinity is our keeper, the Trinity is our everlasting lover, the Trinity is our endless joy and bliss, through our Lord Jesus Christ and in our Lord Jesus Christ. And this was shown to me in the first revelation and in all the others, for wherever Jesus appears the Blessed Trinity is also present.

The strength and the ground of everything was revealed in the first revelation.

RDL ch. 4, ch. 6

Enfolded in Love

God created man in the image of himself,
in the image of God he created him,
male and female he created them.
God blessed them, saying to them,
"Be fruitful, multiply,
fill the earth and conquer it."
God saw all he had made,
and indeed it was very good.

Genesis 1:27-28a, 31a

Prayer: God, in your goodness, give me yourself;
           in you only do I have all I need.

A t the same time as I had the bodily vision of the bleeding head, our good Lord also gave me a spiritual vision of his homely loving. I saw that he is to us everything which is good and comfortable for our help. He is our clothing which for love enwraps us and enfolds us, embraces us and shelters us: and with his tender love he is so close to us that he can never leave us. So I saw in this vision that he is everything that is good.

Then he showed me a little thing, no bigger than a hazelnut as it seemed to me, lying in the palm of my hand, and it was as round as a ball. I looked at it with the eye of my understanding and thought, "What can it be?" And I was answered: "It is all that is made."

I gazed with astonishment, wondering how it could survive, because of its littleness. It seemed to me that it should presently fall into nothingness. And I was answered in my mind: "It lasts and always will last because God loves it." So everything receives its being from the love of God.

We need to be aware of the littleness of created things to avoid being attached to them, and so come to love and possess God who is uncreated.

Our good Lord also showed me that it gives him great pleasure when a helpless soul comes to him openly, plainly and humbly. From this vision I understood that the soul naturally longs to do this through the touch of the Holy Spirit: "God, in your goodness give me yourself, for you are enough for me. I can ask for nothing less if I am truly to live for your glory. If I were to ask for less I would always remain in need. Only in you do I have everything."

RDL ch. 5

The life of man — to know and love God

God, infinitely perfect and blessed in himself, in a plan of sheer goodness freely created man to make him share in his own blessed life. For this reason, at every time and in every place, God draws close to man. He calls man to seek him, to know him, to love him with all his strength.

CCC 1

The desire for God is written in the human heart, because man is created by God and for God; and God never ceases to draw man to himself. Only in God will he find the truth and happiness he never stops searching for . . . forms of religious expression, despite the ambiguities they often bring with them, are so universal that one may well call man a religious being.

CCC 27, 28

Hold Fast to His Goodness

Yahweh, how great your goodness,
reserved for those who fear you,
bestowed on those who take shelter in you,
for all mankind to see!
Blessed be Yahweh, who performs marvels of love for me.
Be strong, let your heart be bold,
all you who hope in Yahweh!

Psalm 31:19, 21, 24

Prayer: Lord, in all my needs lead me to focus
on your goodness and enfold me in it.

This Revelation was given to teach us to wisely hold onto the goodness of God. At the same time our ways of praying were brought to my mind: how in our ignorance of his love we make use of many ways and means. Then I saw very clearly that if we faithfully pray to him with true understanding and steadfast belief, trusting only in his goodness and clinging only to this by the power of his grace, it gives him more glory than if we make use of all the ways and means of which our hearts may think. For if we take all these ways and means, it will be inadequate and will fall short of true worship of God. All that we need lies in his goodness, nothing is missing there.

To centre on the goodness of God is the highest form of prayer, and God's goodness comes to meet us at our most basic need. It gives life to our soul and makes it live and grow in grace and virtue. God's goodness is the nearest to us by nature, and the most ready to bring us grace; for it is the same grace which the soul seeks and ever will, until the day in which we truly know God who has enfolded us all in himself.

Truly our Lover desires that we cling to him with all our might, and to cling evermore to his goodness. For, of all the things the heart could think of, this pleases God most and soonest helps us to prayerfulness.

RDL ch. 6

God reveals his plan of loving goodness

It pleased God, in his goodness and wisdom, to reveal himself and to make known the mystery of his will. His will was that men should have access to the Father, through Christ, the Word made flesh, in the Holy Spirit, and thus become sharers in the divine nature (cf. Eph 1:9; 2:18; 2 Pt 1:4).

CCC 51

God, who "dwells in unapproachable light," wants to communicate his own divine life to the men he freely created, in order to adopt them as his sons in his only-begotten Son (1 Tm 6:16; cf. Eph 1:45). By revealing himself God wishes to make them capable of responding to him, and of knowing him and of loving him far beyond their own natural capacity.

CCC 52

A Love beyond Comprehension

My Beloved lifts up his voice, he says to me,
"Come then, my love, my lovely one, come.
For see, winter is past, the rains are over and gone.
Come then, my love, my lovely one, come.
My dove, hiding in the clefts of the rock,
in the coverts of the cliff,
show me your face,
let me hear your voice;
for your voice is sweet
and your face is beautiful."

Song of Songs 2:10-11, 13b-14

Prayer: My Beloved, seek me and draw me
              into the full wonder of your love.

We are so preciously loved by him who is highest that it is far beyond the comprehension of all creatures. That is to say, no created being can fully know how much, how sweetly and how tenderly our Creator loves us. But, with his grace and his help, we can gaze in endless wonder at the infinitely high, surpassing, immeasurable love which our Lord in his goodness has for us. And so we may reverently ask from our Lord all that we want; for our natural will is to have God, and the good will of God is to have us.

We can never stop wanting to be his and longing for him until we possess him in the fullness of joy. Then we will desire nothing more. He wants us to be completely occupied with knowing and loving him until the time when our longing shall be completely fulfilled in heaven.

This is why this lesson of love was shown, with all that follows from it, as you will see; for the strength and ground of everything was revealed in the first revelation. For of all things, the beholding and loving of the Creator makes the soul seem less in its own eyes, and fills it fully with reverent fear and true humility and with abundant love for our fellow-Christians.

RDL ch. 6

God is love

In the course of its history, Israel was able to discover that God had only one reason to reveal himself to them, a single motive for choosing them from all peoples as his special possession: his sheer gratuitous love (cf. Dt 4:37; 7:8; 10:15). And thanks to the prophets Israel understood that it was again out of love that God never stopped saving them and pardoning their unfaithfulness and sins (cf. Is 43:1-7; Hos 2).

CCC 218

God's love for Israel is compared to a father's love for his son. His love for his people is stronger than a mother's love for her children. God loves his people more than a bridegroom his beloved; his love will be victorious over even the worst infidelities and will extend to his most precious gift: "God so loved the world that he gave his only Son" (Jn 3:16; cf. Hos 11:1; Is 49:14-15).

CCC 219

Seek This Joy and Trust Him for It

Yahweh would speak with Moses face to face,
as a man speaks with his friend.
Moses said to Yahweh,
". . . please show me your ways,
so that I can understand you . . . ."
Yahweh replied, "I myself will go with you,
and I will give you rest."
Yahweh said to Moses,
"Again I will do what you have asked,
because you have won my favour
and because I know you by name."

Exodus 33:11a, 12-14, 17

Prayer: My Friend, be with me in my journeying
              and in my resting to show me your ways.

The greatest honour a great king or a nobleman can bestow upon a poor servant is to treat him as a personal friend, especially if he does it sincerely and wholeheartedly in public and in private. Then the servant will think, "See, what greater honour and joy could this nobleman give me than to show me, who am so little, such wonderful homeliness. Truly, it gives me more joy and pleasure than if he were to give me great gifts, while remaining a stranger to me in his behaviour." This visual example was shown so mightily it was as if the man's heart could be carried away and that he almost forgot himself for joy over this marvellous homeliness.

That's how it stands with our Lord Jesus and us. It seems to me that there can surely be no greater joy than that the one who is highest and mightiest, noblest and most worthy, should also be the one who is most lowly, humble, homely and courteous. And surely and truly he will make this marvellous joy our own when we shall see him. It is our good Lord's

will for us that we believe and trust, enjoy and delight,
comfort and solace ourselves as best we can (with his grace
and his help) until the time when we see him in reality.

It seems to me that the greatest joy we shall ever know
comes from seeing the wonderful courtesy and homeliness of
our Father who is our Creator, and we shall see this in our Lord
Jesus Christ, who is our brother and Saviour.

RDL ch. 7

An eternal exchange of love

God's love is "everlasting" (Is 54:8). "For the mountains may depart and the hills be removed, but my
steadfast love shall not depart from you" (Is 54:10; cf.
54:8). Through Jeremiah, God declares to his people,
"I have loved you with an everlasting love; therefore I
have continued my faithfulness to you" (Jer 31:3).

CCC 220

But John goes even further when he affirms that "God
is love" (1 Jn 4:8,16). God's very being is love. By
sending his only Son and the Spirit of Love in the fullness of time, God has revealed his inner-most secret
(cf. 1 Cor 2:7-16; Eph 3:9-12): God himself is an
eternal exchange of love, Father, Son and Holy Spirit,
and he has destined us to share in that exchange.

CCC 221

Peace and Encouragement for the Simple

Neither the planter nor the waterer matters:
only God, who makes things grow.
It is all one who does the planting and who does the watering,
and each will duly be paid according to his share of the work.
We are fellow workers with God;
you are God's farm, God's building.
For the foundation, nobody can lay any other
than the one which has already been laid,
that is Jesus Christ.

1 Corinthians 3:7-9, 11

Prayer: Lord, may my acceptance of your peace and
          encouragement be a strength for others.

Everything that I am saying about myself I mean to say about all my fellow-Christians, for I was taught in the spiritual vision that this is what our Lord God intends it for. Therefore I beg you all for God's sake, and I advise you for your own benefit, that you stop thinking about the poor wretch to whom the vision was shown, but that you better, powerfully, wisely and humbly contemplate God himself, who in his courteous love and in his endless goodness wanted to show these things to all, so that all may be comforted. It is God's will that you accept it with the greatest joy and delight, as if Jesus himself had shown it to you.

I am not good because of this vision, but only if I love God more because of it. And to the extent that you love God more than I do, you are that much better than I am. I am not saying this to those who are wise, for they know it well enough. But I am saying it to you who are simple, to give you peace and comfort, for we are in fact all one in love. And truly it was not shown to me that God loves me more than the least soul that is in the state of grace. I am sure that there are many who have not had any revelations or visions outside the ordinary teaching of Holy Church and yet who love God better than I do. If I look at myself alone I am nothing at all, but in the whole body of Christ I am, I hope, united in love with all my fellow-Christians.

It is on this union of love that the life of all those who are going to be saved depends. God is all that is good (as I see it) and God has made all that is made and God loves all that he has made. Therefore whoever loves all fellow-Christians as a whole for God's sake, loves all that is made. For in humankind that shall be saved is comprehended all (I mean all that is made and the Maker of all) for God is in us, and in God is all. And he who loves thus, loves all. I hope, by the grace of God, that whoever sees things in this way shall be truly taught and mightily comforted, if in need of comfort.

The faith of Holy Church, which I was taught and have practised since, and which I hope by the grace of God to continue to observe both in use and in custom, was always before my eyes, with the desire and the intention never to accept anything that might be contrary to it.

RDL ch. 8; ch. 9

God has said everything in his Word

"In many and various ways God spoke of old to our fathers by the prophets, but in these last days he has spoken to us by a Son" (Heb 1:1-2). Christ, the Son of God made man, is the Father's one, perfect and unsurpassable Word. In him he has said everything; there will be no other word than this one.

CCC 65

Yet even if Revelation is already complete, it has not been made completely explicit; it remains for Christian faith gradually to grasp its full significance over the course of the centuries.

CCC 66

Throughout the ages, there have been so-called "private" revelations, some of which have been recognised by the authority of the Church. They do not belong, however, to the deposit of faith. It is not their role to improve or complete Christ's definitive Revelation, but to help live more fully by it in a certain period of history. Guided by the Magisterium of the Church, the *sensus fidelium*[1] knows how to discern and welcome in these revelations whatever constitutes an authentic call of Christ or his saints to the Church.

CCC 67

---

1. The *sensus fidelium* refers to the infused sensitivity and discrimination which the faithful, the members of the Church, which is the Body of Christ, possess in matters of belief ("When the Spirit of truth comes he will lead you to the complete truth" — Jn 16:13), guided by the *Magisterium*, the teaching authority of the Church ("All authority has been given to me. Make disciples of all the nations. Teach them to observe all the commands I gave you" — Mt 28:18,19,20).

The Second Revelation

We Need Nothing but God

After this I saw with bodily sight, in the face of the crucifix that hung before me and at which I continually gazed, part of Christ's Passion.

I saw there insults, spittle and dirt, bruises and many long drawn-out pains, more than I can tell, and frequent changes of colour in his face. Then I saw how half of the face, beginning at the ear, was covered with dried blood which formed a kind of crust as far as the middle of the face. After that the other half was covered in the same way. Then it vanished in the first part just as it had come.

This I saw bodily, but it was clouded and dim, and I wanted more light so as to see it more clearly. Then I was answered in my mind: "If God wants to show you more he will be your light. You need nothing but him." For I saw him and I sought him.

We are now so blind and foolish that we are unable to seek God until the time when he in his goodness shows himself to us. And when by grace we do see something of him, we are then moved by that same grace to seek him with even greater longing so as to see him more joyfully.

RDL ch. 10

The Lord's Beauty
Hidden by Our Shame

As the crowds were appalled on seeing him
— so disfigured did he look that he seemed no longer human —
so will the crowds be astonished at him,
and kings stand speechless before him;
for they shall see something never told
and witness something never heard before.
Without beauty, without majesty (we saw him),
no looks to attract our eyes.
Yet he was pierced through for our faults, crushed for our sins.
On him lies a punishment that brings us peace,
and through his wounds we are healed.

Isaiah 52:14-15; 53:2b, 5

Prayer: Lord, that I may imitate you,
              re-created in your image and likeness.

This second Revelation was so modest, so ordinary and so simple, that my spirit was deeply disturbed by the beholding of it; passing from grief, to fear, to longing, because for some time I doubted whether it was a revelation at all. Then at various times our good Lord gave me greater insight so that I now know for certain that this was a revelation. It symbolised and represented our death, foul and black, which our blessed Lord, fair and radiant, suffered for our sins.

We know from our faith and from the teaching and preaching of Holy Church that the Blessed Trinity made humankind in his image and likeness. Similarly, we know that when man fell so deeply and so wretchedly through sin, there was no other help to restore him save through the One who created him. And he who created man for love, by that same love wanted to restore man to the same blessedness, and even more. And just as we were made like the Trinity in our first making, so our Creator wanted us to be like our Saviour Jesus Christ in heaven and live there forever by the power of our re-creation.

Then, between these two creations, out of love and respect for man he wanted to make himself as much like man in this mortal life, with all its wretchedness and filth, as could be possible but without sin. This is what I meant earlier when I said that it was the image and likeness of our death, foul and black, in which our fair and radiant Lord hid his Godhead. There has never been a man more beautiful than the Lord Jesus until the time when his beauty was scarred by his suffering, his sorrow, his Passion and his death.

RDL ch. 10

The mission of the Trinity

God is eternal blessedness, undying life, unfading light. God is love: Father, Son and Holy Spirit. God freely wills to communicate the glory of his blessed life. Such is the "plan of his loving kindness," conceived by the Father before the foundation of the world, in his beloved Son: "He destined us in love to be his sons" and "to be conformed to the image of his Son," through "the spirit of sonship" (Eph 1:4-5,9; Rom 8:15,29). This plan is a "grace [which] was given to us in Christ Jesus before the ages began," stemming immediately from Trinitarian love (2 Tm 1:9-10). It unfolds in the work of creation, the whole history of salvation after the fall, and the missions of the Son and the Spirit, which are continued in the mission of the Church.

CCC 257

Seeking Him until We See Him

God, you are my God, I am seeking you,
my soul is thirsting for you, my flesh is longing for you,
a land parched, weary and waterless;
I long to gaze on you in the Sanctuary,
and to see your power and glory.

Psalm 63:1-2

Prayer: Lord, teach me to seek you and to trust you completely
in every circumstance.

This vision taught me to see that it is greatly pleasing to God
when the soul continually seeks him. In fact it cannot do
more than seek, suffer and trust.

This itself is the work of the Holy Spirit in the soul. And
the brilliance of finding him comes from the Spirit's special
grace, when it is his will. Seeking with faith, hope and love
pleases our Lord, and finding him pleases the soul and fills it
full of joy. And so I was made to understand that seeking is as
good as beholding during the time that God allows the soul to
be in turmoil. It is God's will that we go on seeking him until
we see him, for it is because of this that he will show himself to
us in his special grace when he so wills.

God himself will teach the soul how to behave itself in
beholding him. This is what brings most glory to him and is
most helpful to the soul, making it most open to receive
humility and other virtues by the grace and guidance of the
Holy Spirit. For a soul that does nothing but hold onto God
with absolute trust, either by seeking him or in beholding him
is, it seems to me, offering to him the greatest honour
possible.

RDL ch. 10

Trusting God in every circumstance

Believing in God, the only One, and loving him with all our being has enormous consequences for our whole life.

It means coming to know God's greatness and majesty: "Behold, God is great, and we know him not" (Jb 36:26). Therefore, we must "serve God first."[1]

It means living in thanksgiving: if God is the only One, everything we are and have comes from him: "What have you that you did not receive?" (1 Cor 4:7). "What shall I render to the Lord for all his bounty to me?" (Ps 116:12).

It means knowing the unity and true dignity of all men: everyone is made in the image and likeness of God (Gn 1:26).

It means making good use of created things: faith in God, the only One, leads us to use everything that is not God only insofar as it brings us closer to him, and to detach ourselves from it insofar as it turns us away from him.

It means trusting God in every circumstance, even in adversity.

                                        CCC 222-227

---

1. St. Joan of Arc; said by her before her judges at her trial in 1431 when insisting that before all else "God must be served first."

Seeking Is Open to Everyone

I know the plans I have in mind for you
— it is Yahweh who speaks —
plans for peace, not disaster,
reserving a future full of hope for you.
Then when you call to me, and come to plead with me,
I will listen to you.
When you seek me, you shall find me,
when you seek me with all your heart;
I will let you find me.

Jeremiah 29:11-14a

Prayer: Abba Father, that in seeking I may find,
that in faith I may have utter trust.

There are the two activities that can be seen in this vision: one is seeking, the other is beholding. The seeking is common to all; that is to say, every soul can do it with the help of God's grace, making use of discernment and following the teaching of Holy Church.

It is the will of God that we have in our seeking three things as a gift from him. The first is that through his grace we seek willingly and diligently and without sloth, as far as we can; gladly and happily, without unreasonable sadness and useless sorrow. The second is that we wait for him steadfastly out of love for him, without grumbling and striving against him, until (which cannot be far away) our life's end. The third is that we trust him utterly out of complete faith in him, for he wants us to know that he will appear suddenly and blessedly to all who love him.

His work is done in secret, yet he wants to be perceived; and his appearing will be very sudden. And he wants to be trusted, for he is so homely and courteous. Blessed may he be!

RDL ch. 10

Faith in an almighty Father

God is the Father Almighty, whose fatherhood and power shed light on one another: God reveals his fatherly omnipotence by the way he takes care of our needs; by the filial adoption that he gives us ("I will be a father to you, and you shall be my sons and daughters, says the Almighty") (2 Cor 6:18; cf. Mt 6:32): finally by his infinite mercy, for he displays his power at its height by freely forgiving sins.

CCC 270

Faith in God the Father Almighty can be put to the test by the experience of evil and suffering. God can sometimes seem to be absent and incapable of stopping evil.[2] But in the most mysterious way God the Father has revealed his almighty power in the voluntary humiliation and Resurrection of his Son, by which he conquered evil. Christ crucified is thus "the power of God and the wisdom of God. For the foolishness of God is wiser than men, and the weakness of God is stronger than men" (1 Cor 1:24-25). It is in Christ's Resurrection and exaltation that the Father has shown forth "the immeasurable greatness of his power in us who believe" (Eph 1:19-22).

CCC 272

---

2. The reader who is troubled by the question — "If God is good, why does he permit so much evil and suffering?" — will find profound reassurance in the classic *The Problem of Pain* by C S Lewis (1898-1963), an Anglican writer gifted with an exceptionally brilliant, logical and pastoral mind, expressing Christian truths in a common-sense manner accessible to those of many outlooks. (*The Problem of Pain*, C S Lewis, Fount Paperbacks, HarperCollinsReligious, London, 1977.)

The
Third
Revelation

God Our Lord Does All

After this I saw God in a point[1] that is to say, in my mind's eye — by which vision I saw that he is in all things.

I looked at it carefully, seeing and recognising through it that he does all that is done. I marvelled at this vision with a slight fear, and I thought, "What is sin?"

For I saw truly that God does all things, however small they may be. And I saw very clearly that nothing is done by chance or luck, but all is done by the foreseeing wisdom of God. If it seems like chance or luck in our eyes, the reason for that it is our blindness and lack of foresight. For those things which are in God's foreseeing wisdom from all eternity, and which he so rightly and to his glory continually brings to their best conclu-

---

1. This mystical expression refers to God's unity, perfection and infiniteness; the first cause from whom all creation flows and in whom it has its being. "God is the centre of everything and he does everything," Julian states (ch. 11, p. 25). This understanding is, of course, quite distinct from and opposed to the pantheist idea that God is everything and everything God. Relevantly, the (Eastern) Orthodox Tradition distinguishes between God's essence (absolute divine transcendence), remaining hidden and unapproachable outside his creation; and his energies (divine immanence), God himself permeating his creation, coming down to us and acting in concrete circumstances.

sion, seem to fall on us out of the blue, catching us unawares. So, in our blindness and lack of foresight we say, "It's all luck and chance." But to our Lord it is not so.

This compelled me to admit that everything that is done is done well, for God our Lord does all. At this time I was not shown the working of God's creatures, only the working of God in his creatures.

RDL ch. 11

There Is No Doer but God

For anyone who is in Christ, there is a new creation;
the old creation has gone, and now the new one is here.
It is all God's work.
It was God who reconciled us to himself through Christ
and gave us the work of handing on this reconciliation.
In other words, God in Christ was reconciling the world to himself,
not holding men's faults against them,
and he has entrusted to us the news that they are reconciled.
So we are ambassadors for Christ;
it is as though God were appealing through us.

2 Corinthians 5:17-20a

Prayer: Lord Jesus, that I may be your ambassador
of reconciliation, your creative co-worker.

This vision was shown to teach me that our Lord wants us to turn around and sincerely contemplate him and all his works. For they are totally good, and all his decrees are easy and sweet. They bring great peace to the soul that has turned away from contemplating the blind pronouncements of mortals to focus on the lovely and delightful decrees of our Lord God. A person may see some deeds are done well and others are evil, but our Lord does not see them like this.[2] For just as all that exists in nature is the work of God so likewise all deeds bear the stamp of God's doing. It is easy to understand that the best of deeds is done well; but the most insig-

---

2. Julian is not in this phrase discussing God's actions ("for they are totally good") but the individual's harsh, even despairing, "blind pronouncements" in judgement of his or her self, in which the individual overlooks the totality of God's salvific action which will turn all harm into utter good. You are not your own property; you have been bought and paid for (1 Cor 6:19-20). Therefore I will not even pass judgement on myself (1 Cor 4:3); then "all deeds bear the stamp of God's doing. . . . For there is no doer but God."

nificant deed that is being done is done just as well as the best and the greatest. Everything is according to the quality and in the order ordained by God even before the world began. For there is no doer but God.

RDL ch. 11

God carries out his plan: divine providence

Creation has its own goodness and proper perfection, but it did not spring forth complete from the hands of the Creator. The universe was created "in a state of journeying" (in statu viae) toward an ultimate perfection yet to be attained, to which God has destined it. We call "divine providence" the dispositions by which God guides his creation toward this perfection.

CCC 302

Jesus asks for childlike abandonment to the providence of our heavenly Father who takes care of his children's smallest needs: "Therefore do not be anxious, saying, 'What shall we eat?' or 'What shall we drink?' . . . Your heavenly Father knows that you need them all. But seek first his kingdom and his righteousness, and all these things shall be yours as well" (Mt 6:31-33; cf. 10:29-31).

CCC 305

To human beings God even gives the power of freely sharing in his providence by entrusting them with the responsibility of "subduing" the earth and having dominion over it (cf. Gn 1:26-28). God thus enables men to be intelligent and free causes in order to complete the work of creation, to perfect its harmony for their own good and that of their neighbours.

CCC 307

God Does All Things

Before God, we are confident of this through Christ:
not that we are qualified in ourselves to claim anything
as our own work:
all our qualifications come from God.
We are only the earthenware jars that hold this treasure,
to make it clear that such an overwhelming power comes from
*   God and not from us.*
We are in difficulties on all sides, but never cornered;
we see no answer to our problems, but never despair;
we have been persecuted, but never deserted;
knocked down, but never killed;
always, wherever we may be, we carry with us in our body
the death of Jesus,
so that the life of Jesus, too, may be seen in our body.

2 Corinthians 3:4-5; 4:7-10

Prayer: Lord Jesus, that in sharing your death with you,
         I may share your life with others.

I saw with absolute certainly that God never changes his purpose in anything, nor ever will. For there was nothing unknown to him in his rightful ordering of things from the very beginning. Therefore everything was set in order before anything was made so that it would endure for ever. And no manner of thing will fall short of God's plan for it because he has made all things perfectly good.

And therefore the Blessed Trinity is always fully pleased with all his work. God revealed all this to me with great happiness as if to say: "See, I am God. See, I am in all things. See, I do all things. See, I never lift my hands from my works, nor ever shall without end. See, I guide all things to the end that I planned for them before time began, and I do it with the same power and wisdom and love with which I made them. How can anything be amiss?"

In this way, powerfully, wisely and lovingly, was my soul tested through this vision. Then I saw truly that I could do nothing else but assent to it with great reverence and joy in God.

RDL ch. 11

Why did God not create a world so perfect that no evil could exist in it?

Angels and men, as intelligent and free creatures, have to journey toward their ultimate destinies by their free choice and preferential love. They can therefore go astray. Indeed, they have sinned. Thus has moral evil, incommensurably more harmful than physical evil, entered the world. God is in no way, directly or indirectly, the cause of moral evil. He permits it, however, because he respects the freedom of his creatures and, mysteriously, knows how to derive good from it. For almighty God, because he is supremely good, would never allow any evil whatsoever to exist in his works if he were not so all-powerful and good as to cause good to emerge from evil itself.

CCC 311

We firmly believe that God is master of the world and of its history. But the ways of his providence are often unknown to us. Only at the end, when our partial knowledge ceases, when we see God "face to face" (1 Cor 13:12), will we fully know the ways by which — even through the dramas of evil and sin — God has guided his creation to that definitive Sabbath rest (cf. Gn 2:2) for which he created heaven and earth.

CCC 314

The Fourth Revelation

Christ's Blood Washes Us Clean

After this, as I looked, I saw the body bleeding heavily, apparently from the flogging. The smooth skin was gashed and all over his body I saw deep weals in the tender flesh caused by many sharp blows. The blood flowed so hot and thick that neither the wounds nor the skin could be seen: it was all covered in blood. The blood flowed all down his body, but at the point of falling to the ground, it disappeared. The bleeding continued for a while, giving me time to see it and think about it. It was so heavy that I thought that if it had been real the whole bed and everything around would have been soaked in blood.

RDL ch. 12

His Holy Blood Washes Us Clean from Our Sins

"I tell you most solemnly,
if you do not eat the flesh of the Son of Man
and drink his blood,
you will not have life in you.
Anyone who does eat my flesh and drink my blood
has eternal life,
and I shall raise him up on the last day.
For my flesh is real food
and my blood is real drink.
He who eats my flesh and drinks my blood
lives in me
and I live in him."

John 6:53-56

How much more effectively the blood of Christ,
who offered himself as the perfect sacrifice to God
through the eternal Spirit,
can purify our inner self from dead actions
so that we do our service to the living God.

Hebrews 9:14

Prayer: Lord, I am not worthy to receive you,
but only say the word and I shall be healed.

The dear worthy blood of our Lord Jesus Christ is truly as plentiful as it is most precious. Behold and see the power of this precious abundance of his dear worthy blood. It descended down into hell, burst hell's chains and freed all who were there who belonged to the court of heaven. The precious abundance of his dear worthy blood flows over the whole world ready to wash away all sin from every human being who is of good will, who has been and shall be. The precious abundance of his dear worthy blood rises up to heaven in the blessed body of our Lord Jesus Christ, and there it is now within him, bleeding and praying for us to the Father. That is how it is now and shall be as long as we have need of it. And even more it flows through all heaven, rejoicing at the salvation of all people who are already there and those who are still to come, thus completing the appointed number of the saints.

RDL ch. 12

Thanksgiving and praise to the Father

The Eucharist is a sacrifice of thanksgiving to the Father, a blessing by which the Church expresses her gratitude to God for all his benefits, for all that he has accomplished through creation, redemption and sanctification. Eucharist means first of all "thanksgiving."

CCC 1360

Because it is the memorial of Christ's Passover, the Eucharist is also a sacrifice. The sacrificial character of the Eucharist is manifested in the very words of institution: "This is my body which is given for you" and "This cup which is poured out for you is the New Covenant in my blood" (Lk 22:19-20). In the Eucharist Christ gives us the very body which he gave up for us on the cross, the very blood which he "poured out for many for the forgiveness of sins" (Mt 26:28).

CCC 1365

In the most blessed sacrament of the Eucharist the body and blood, together with the soul and divinity, of our Lord Jesus Christ and, therefore, the whole Christ is truly, really, and substantially contained. This presence is called "real" — by which is not intended to exclude the other types of presence as if they could not be "real" too, but because it is presence in the fullest sense: that is to say, it is a substantial presence by which Christ, God and man, makes himself wholly and entirely present.

CCC 1374

Holy Communion augments our union with Christ. The principal fruit of receiving the Eucharist in Holy Communion is an intimate union with Christ Jesus. Indeed the Lord said: "He who eats my flesh and drinks my blood abides in me, and I in him" (Jn 6:56).

CCC 1391

The
Fifth
Revelation

The Defeat of Evil

After this, before speaking to me, God gave me time to reflect on him and all that I had seen and all that it meant as far as my simple soul could take it in. Then, without voice or speech, he gave these words to my soul:

"With this the devil is overcome."

These words our Lord said in reference to his blessed Passion as he had shown me earlier.

RDL ch. 13

The Power of Christ's Precious Passion

Then Jesus was led by the Spirit out into the wilderness to be
tempted by the devil. He fasted for forty days and forty nights, after
which he was very hungry, and the tempter came and said to him,
"If you are the Son of God, tell these stones to turn into loaves."
But he replied, "Scripture says: Man does not live on bread alone
but on every word that comes from the mouth of God."
Next, taking him to a very high mountain, the devil showed him
all the kingdoms of the world and their splendour.
"I will give you all these" he said, "if you fall at my feet
and worship me."
Then Jesus replied, "Be off, Satan! For scripture says:
You must worship the Lord your God, and serve him alone."
Then the devil left him, and angels appeared and looked after him.

Matthew 4:1-4, 8-11

Prayer: Lord, that I may endure, be my strength;
           my eternal joy, be my reward at the end.

In this our Lord showed a part of the devil's malice together
with all his impotence, because he showed me that his
Passion is overcoming the devil.[1] God showed me that the

---

1. The name *Devil* is from the Greek *diabolos,* meaning *slanderer, accuser, enemy* — "the persecutor, who accused our brothers day and night before our God" (Rv 13:10). Now also known as Satan (from the Hebrew *satan,* meaning *enemy* or *plotter*), he is identified, before his rebellion and fall, with the angel of God named Lucifer (from the Latin *light-bearer*), a name shared with the planet Venus when it rises as the morning star. So, the reference in Isaiah 14:12-15; "How did you come to fall from the heavens, Daystar, son of Dawn? How did you come to be thrown to the ground, you who enslaved the nations? You who used to think to yourself , 'I will climb up to the heavens. . . . I will rival the Most High.' What! You have fallen to Sheol to the very bottom of the abyss!" Having blasphemously sought to rival God, he seeks to tempt and enslave mankind in his presumptuous plotting to gain that power which belongs only to God — it was the serpent Satan in the Garden who said, "No! You will not die! God knows that on the day you eat it your eyes will be opened and you will become like gods . . ." (Gn 3:5).

devil is now just as malicious as he was before the Incarnation and that, however hard he works, he sees that just as before all the souls destined to be saved gloriously escape him by virtue of Christ's precious Passion. This is the devil's sorrow and shameful horror, because everything which God permits him to do turns to joy for us and rebounds on him in disgrace and pain. And his sorrow is just as great when God permits him to work as when he does not work. This is because he can never do all the evil he wants to do, for his power is all locked in God's hands. But in God there is no anger, as I see it.

I also saw our Lord scorn the devil's malice, and reduce his empty power to nothing; and he wants us to do the same. For I saw that on Judgement Day he will be generally scorned by all who shall be saved, and whose salvation he greatly resents. Then he will see that all the woe and tribulation that he has brought them have served only to increase their eternal joy. And all the pain and the sorrow that he would have led them into will for ever go with him into hell.

RDL ch. 13

Freedom put to the test

God created man in his image and established him in his friendship. A spiritual creature, man can live this friendship only in free submission to God. Man is dependent on his Creator, and subject to the laws of creation and to the moral norms that govern the use of freedom.

CCC 396

Man, tempted by the devil, let his trust in his Creator die in his heart and, abusing his freedom, disobeyed God's command. This is what man's first sin consisted of (cf. Gn 3:1-11; Rom 5:19). All subsequent sin would be disobedience toward God and lack of trust in his goodness.

CCC 397

Scripture portrays the tragic consequences of this first disobedience. Adam and Eve immediately lose the grace of original holiness (cf. Rom 3:23). They become afraid of the God of whom they have conceived a distorted image — that of a God jealous of his prerogatives (cf. Gn 3:5-10).

CCC 399

The power of Satan is, nonetheless, not infinite. He is only a creature, powerful from the fact that he is pure spirit, but still a creature. He cannot prevent the building up of God's reign. Although Satan may act in the world out of hatred for God and his kingdom in Christ Jesus, and although his action may cause grave injuries — of a spiritual nature and, indirectly, even of a physical nature — to each man and to society, the action is permitted by divine providence which with strength and gentleness guides human and cosmic history. It is a great mystery that providence should permit diabolical activity, but "we know that in everything God works for good with those who love him" (Rom 8:28).

CCC 395

The
Sixth
Revelation

Everlasting Life

After this our Lord said: "Thank you for your service and your dedication in your youth."

With this my spirit was lifted up into heaven where I saw our Lord God as the Lord of his own house, who has called all his dear worthy servants and friends to a great feast.

RDL ch. 14

A Fullness of Joy and Happiness

In my vision, I heard the sound of an immense number of angels
gathered round the throne and the animals and the elders;
there were ten thousand times ten thousand of them
and thousands upon thousands, shouting,
"The Lamb that was sacrificed is worthy to be given
power, riches, wisdom, strength, honour, glory and blessing."
Then I heard all the living things in creation —
everything that lives in the air, and on the ground,
and under the ground, and in the sea, crying,
"To the One who is sitting on the throne and to the Lamb,
be all praise, honour, glory and power, for ever and ever."
And the four animals said, "Amen";
and the elders prostrated themselves in worship.

Revelation 5:11-14

Prayer: Lamb of God, all praise, honor, power and glory
be yours in heaven and on earth.

Then I saw that the Lord was not seated in any special place in his own house, but I saw him preside like a king over everything, filling the whole house with joy and mirth. He continually comforted his beloved friends and made them glad with his homeliness and courteousness, and with the marvellous melody of eternal love in his beautiful, blessed face. This glorious face of the Godhead fills all the heavens full of joy and bliss.

God showed me the three degrees of bliss that every soul will enjoy in heaven who has willingly served God in any way here on earth. The first is the honour and gratitude of our Lord God which the soul will receive when it is set free from suffering. It seemed to me that all the pain and suffering that could ever be endured by all the living could not deserve the wonderful gratitude that one person will receive who has freely served God.

The second degree is that all the blessed creatures that are in heaven will see that wonderful gratitude as God tells everyone in heaven about that person's service for him.

The third degree of bliss is that the freshness and joy with which the soul receives the gratitude in the beginning will remain for ever.

RDL ch. 14

Faith — the beginning of eternal life

Faith makes us taste in advance the light of the beatific vision, the goal of our journey here below. Then we shall see God "face to face," "as he is" (1 Cor 13:12; 1 Jn 3:2). So faith is already the beginning of eternal life. When we contemplate the blessings of faith even now, as if gazing at a reflection in a mirror, it is as if we already possessed the wonderful things which our faith assures us we shall one day enjoy.

CCC 163

Now, however, "we walk by faith, not by sight" (2 Cor 5:7); we perceive God as "in a mirror, dimly" and only "in part" (1 Cor 13:12). Even though enlightened by him in whom it believes, faith is often lived in darkness and can be put to the test.

CCC 164

It is then we must turn to the witnesses of faith: to Abraham, who "in hope . . . believed against hope" (Rom 4:18); to the Virgin Mary, who, in her pilgrimage of faith, walked into the night of faith in sharing the darkness of her son's suffering and death; and to so many others: "Therefore, since we are surrounded by so great a cloud of witnesses, let us also lay aside every weight, and sin which clings so closely, and let us run with perseverance the race that is set before us, looking to Jesus the pioneer and perfecter of our faith" (Heb 12:1-2).

CCC 165

The Reward for the Intention to Serve God for Ever

Since you have been brought back to true life with Christ,
you must look for the things that are in heaven,
where Christ is, sitting at God's right hand.
Let your thoughts be on heavenly things,
not on the things that are on the earth,
because you have died,
and now the life you have is hidden with Christ in God.
But when Christ is revealed — and he is your life —
you too will be revealed
in all your glory with him.

Colossians 3:1-4

Prayer: Lord, reveal your life in mine; be my eyes, tongue, hands and feet in your service.

I also saw that in heaven everyone's age will be known and everyone will be rewarded for their willing service and for the length of their service. Those who willingly and freely offer their youth to God are most fittingly rewarded and wonderfully thanked. But I saw that whenever or at whatever time a man or woman truly turns to God, with full intention to serve him (even if that service should last only one day) he or she would experience all three degrees of bliss. The more the loving soul sees this kindness of God, the more willing it is to serve him all the days of its life.

RDL ch. 14

The freedom and the revealings of faith

For a Christian, believing in God cannot be separated from believing in the One he sent, his "beloved Son," in whom the Father is "well pleased"; God tells us to listen to him (Mk 1:11; cf. 9:7). The Lord himself said to his disciples: "Believe in God, believe also in me" (Jn 14:1). We can believe in Jesus Christ because he is himself God, the Word made flesh: "No one has ever seen God; the only Son, who is in the bosom of the Father, he has made him known" (Jn 1:18). Because he "has seen the Father," Jesus Christ is the only one who knows him and can reveal him (Jn 6:46; cf. Mt 11:27).

CCC 151

Believing is possible only by grace and the interior helps of the Holy Spirit. But it is no less true that believing is an authentically human act. Trusting in God and cleaving to the truths he has revealed is contrary neither to human freedom nor to human reason. Even in human relations it is not contrary to our dignity to believe what other persons tell us about themselves and their intentions, or to trust their promises (for example, when a man and a woman marry) to share a communion of life with one another. If this is so, still less is it contrary to our dignity to yield by faith the full submission of intellect and will to God who reveals, and to share an interior communion with him.

CCC 154

The
Seventh
Revelation

Everlasting Bliss

After this God infused into my soul a most wonderful spiritual delight. I was completely filled with an awareness of everlasting security in which I was powerfully sustained without any painful fear. This feeling was so glad and so spiritual that I was totally at peace, at ease and at rest, so that there was nothing on earth that could have grieved me.

RDL ch. 15

Do Not Dwell on Sadness

Nothing therefore can come between us and the love of Christ,
even if we are troubled or worried, or being persecuted,
or lacking food or clothes, or being threatened or even attacked.
As scripture promised:
For your sake we are being massacred daily,
and reckoned as sheep for the slaughter.
These are the trials through which we triumph,
by the power of him who loved us.
For I am certain of this: neither death nor life,
no angel, no prince, nothing that exists, nothing still to come,
not any power, or height or depth, nor any created thing,
can ever come between us and the love of God
made visible in Christ Jesus our Lord.

Romans 8:35-39

Prayer: Lord, in bad and good times alike, grant me grace
to hold onto your endless joy.

This state lasted only for a short while, then all changed. I was left all alone, deeply depressed and tired of my life, so weary of myself I could hardly bear to go on living. There was no comfort or calm for me now, only faith, hope and love; and these I did not feel, I only believed they were true.

Then soon after this our blessed Lord once again gave me comfort and rest for my soul. This was so satisfying and certain, so blissfully happy and powerful, that no fear, no sorrow, no physical or spiritual pain of any kind could upset me. Then again I felt the pain, and then again the delight and joy. Now one, now the other, repeatedly, I suppose about twenty times. In the times of joy I could have said with Paul: "Nothing shall separate me from the love of Christ," and in the pain I could have said with Peter: "Lord, save me, I am perishing."

I understood that this vision was shown to teach me that it is good for some souls to feel like this — up in the air, then down in the dumps: sometimes strengthened, sometimes desolate and abandoned. God wants us to know that he keeps us always safe in bad and good times alike. Sometimes we are left to ourselves for the good of our souls, even though our sin is not always the cause of it. For at this time I committed no sin for which I should have been left to myself — it all happened too quickly. On the other hand, neither did I deserve these blissful feelings of joy. But our Lord gives freely whenever he wills, and sometimes he allows us to be in sorrow. Both states are from one and the same love. Therefore it is not God's will that we dwell on the painful feelings, and grieve and mourn over them. He wants us to pass over them quickly, and keep ourselves in the endless delight which is God.

RDL ch. 15

The consequences of Adam's sin for humanity

All men are implicated in Adam's sin, as Paul affirms: "By one man's disobedience many (that is, all men) were made sinners": "sin came into the world through one man and death through sin, and so death spread to all men because all men sinned . . ." (Rom 5:12, 19). The Apostle contrasts the universality of sin and death with the universality of salvation in Christ. "Then as one man's trespass led to condemnation for all men, so one man's act of righteousness leads to acquittal and life for all men" (Rom 5:18).

CCC 402

Although it is proper to each individual, original sin does not have the character of a personal fault in any of Adam's descendants.[1] It is a deprivation of original holiness and justice, but human nature has not been totally corrupted: it is wounded in the natural powers proper to it, subject to ignorance, suffering and the dominion of death, and inclined to sin — an inclination to evil that is called "concupiscence". Baptism, by imparting the life of Christ's grace, erases original sin and turns a man back towards God, but the consequences for nature, weakened and inclined to evil, persist in man and summon him to spiritual battle.

CCC 405

Thus Paul says, "Where sin increased, grace abounded all the more" (Rom 5:20); and the Exsultet sings, "O happy fault ... which gained for us so great a Redeemer!"

CCC 412

---

1. To avoid confusion about original sin, it is worthwhile stressing in summary the Church's teaching that original sin is a state of the person, not an act, and so not to be confused with personal sin. As Adam (Hebrew *a-dam*, mankind) himself received original holiness and justice for all subsequent human nature, so his commitment of a personal sin in yielding to temptation led to a fallen state (loss of intimacy with God) of human nature — deprived of original holiness and therefore wounded and weakened, variable in states of mind and dispositions. It follows from this that not all our bleak moods are the result of any specific personal sin, but may arise from our sin-wounded condition. At such times we should remain centered on Christ, not changing the good decision taken in good times, but staying determined in our choice of him, sustained by his graces. Surely that is why Julian writes elsewhere (RDL ch. 39) that in heaven, healed of sorrow and suffering, we shall wear the scars caused by sin as marks of honour, trophies of vanquished sin.

The
Eighth
Revelation

Christ's Passion:
The Source of Joy

After this Christ showed me something of his Passion near to the time of his death.

I saw his sweet face all dry and bloodless with the pallor of death, and then later deadly pale, pining away. At last, when death came, his face turned blue, and finally a brownish-blue, as the flesh became more profoundly dead. For his Passion showed itself to me most vividly in his blessed face and especially in his lips. I saw these four colours in his dear face, which I had seen before so fresh, ruddy, healthy and lovely. It was a painful change to see this deep dying.

RDL ch. 16

Choosing Jesus for My Heaven

Jesus said:
"I am the Way, the Truth and the Life.
No one can come to the Father except through me.
If you know me, you know my Father too.
From this moment you know him and have seen him.
To have seen me is to have seen the Father,
so how can you say, 'Let us see the Father'?"

John 14:6-7, 9b

May you have more and more grace and peace
as you come to know our Lord more and more.
By his divine power, he has given us
all the things we need for life and for true devotion,
bringing us to know God himself,
who has called us by his own glory and goodness.
In making these gifts, he has given us the guarantee
of something very great and wonderful to come:
through them you will be able
to share the divine nature
and to escape corruption
in a world which is sunk in vice.

2 Peter 1:2-4

Prayer: Jesus, I choose you for my heaven,
through thick and thin.

A t this time I was tempted to look away from the Cross, but I dared not, because I knew quite well that while I gazed at the Cross I was secure and safe. Therefore I did not want to give in to this desire and put my soul in danger, for apart from the Cross there is no safety from the terror of demons. A suggestion came to my mind in an apparently friendly manner: "Look up to heaven to his Father". With the faith I had I saw clearly that there was nothing between the

Cross and heaven that could have harmed me. I had therefore either to look up or else refuse to do so. I answered inwardly with all the power of my soul, saying: "No, I cannot, for you are my heaven". I said this because I did not want to look up. I would rather have remained in that pain until Judgement Day than enter heaven in any other way than through Jesus.

In this way I was taught to choose Jesus for my heaven; Jesus, whom I saw only in pain at that time. I wanted no other heaven than Jesus, who will be my bliss when I get there. It has always been a great comfort to me that by his grace I chose Jesus to be my heaven throughout all this time of his Passion and sorrow. This has taught me that I should always do so, choosing only Jesus to be my heaven, through thick and thin.

RDL ch. 19

Sharing, by knowledge and love, in God's own life

God has now spoken all at once by giving us the All Who is His Son. Any person questioning God would be guilty not only of foolish behaviour but also of offending him, by not fixing the eyes entirely upon Christ.[1]

CCC 65

Of all visible creatures only man is able to know and love his Creator. He is the only creature on earth that God has willed for its own sake, and he alone is called to share, by knowledge and love, in God's own life. It was for this end that he was created, and this is the fundamental reason for his dignity: "What made you establish man in so great a dignity? Certainly the

---

1. From John of the Cross, commenting upon Hebrews 1:1-2.

incalculable love by which you have looked on your creature in yourself! You are taken with love for her; for by love indeed you created her, by love you have given her a being capable of tasting your eternal Good."[2]

CCC 356

Being in the image of God the human individual possesses the dignity of a person, who is not just something, but someone. He is capable of self-knowledge, of self-possession and of freely giving himself and entering communion with other persons. And he is called by grace to a covenant with his Creator, to offer him a response of faith and love that no other creature can give in his stead.

CCC 357

Christ's Passion Turns All Pain into Joy

In the beginning was the Word:
the Word was with God
and the Word was God.
The Word was made flesh,
he lived among us,
and we saw his glory,
the glory that is his as the only Son of the Father,
full of grace and truth.
No one has ever seen God;
it is the only Son, who is nearest to the Father's heart,
who has made him known.

John 1:1, 14, 18

---

2. Catherine of Siena, *Dialogue* IV, 13.

Prayer: Lord, thank you for choosing to suffer for me,
           and for sharing your joy with me.

Now, the most important point we have to consider in his Passion is to think and to register in our mind that he who suffered is God; and then to reflect on these other two points — one is, what he suffered, and the other is, for whom he suffered.

And in this vision God brought to my mind something of the sublimity and nobility of the glorious Godhead, and at the same time the preciousness and tenderness of his blessed body which is united to it; and how we human creatures hate to suffer pain. For just as he was the most tender and most pure of all people, so he was the one who suffered most deeply and intensely. He suffered for the sins of everyone who shall be saved; and he saw and grieved for everyone's sorrow, desolation and anguish, out of kindness and love. As long as he was capable of suffering he suffered for us and grieved for us. Now he has risen again and so can no longer suffer. Yet he still suffers with us, as I shall explain later.

And as I, by his grace, contemplated all this, I saw that Christ's love for our souls was so strong that he deliberately chose to suffer, indeed with a great desire, and endured all the suffering gently and joyfully.

When a soul touched by grace looks at it like this, it shall truly see that the pains of Christ's Passion surpass all other pains; that is, all pains which will be turned into everlasting and supreme joy by the power of Christ's Passion.

                                                    RDL ch. 20

Christ's offering to the Father, for all

After agreeing to baptise him along with the sinners, John the Baptist looked at Jesus and pointed him out as the "Lamb of God, who takes away the sin of the world" (Jn 1:29; cf. Lk 3:21; Mt 3:14-15; Jn 1:36). By doing so, he reveals that Jesus is at the same time the suffering Servant who silently allows himself to be led to the slaughter and who bears the sins of the multitudes, and also the Paschal Lamb, the symbol of Israel's redemption at the first Passover (Is 53:7,12; cf. Jer 11:19; Ex 12:3-14; Jn 19:36; 1 Cor 5:7). Christ's whole life expresses his mission: "to serve, and to give his life as a ransom for many" (Mk 10:45).

CCC 608

By embracing in his human heart the Father's love for men, Jesus "loved them to the end," for "greater love has no man than this, that a man lay down his life for his friends" (Jn 13:1; 15:13). In suffering and death his humanity became the free and perfect instrument of his divine love which desires the salvation of men (cf. Heb 2:10, 17-18; 4:15; 5:7-9). Indeed, out of love for his Father and for men, whom the Father wants to save, Jesus freely accepted his Passion and death: "No one takes [my life] from me, but I lay it down of my own accord" (Jn 10:18). Hence the sovereign freedom of God's Son as he went out to his death (cf. Jn 18:46; Mt 26:53).

CCC 609

We Shall All Be Brought into Joy

Then I saw a new heaven and a new earth;
the first heaven and the first earth had disappeared now,
and there was no longer any sea.
I saw the holy city, and the new Jerusalem,
coming down from God out of heaven,
as beautiful as a bride all dressed for her husband.
Then I heard a loud voice call from the throne,
"You see this city? Here God lives among men.
He will make his home among them;
they shall be his people,
and he will be their God; his name is God-with-them.
He will wipe away all tears from their eyes;
there will be no more death,
and no more mourning or sadness.
The world of the past has gone."

Revelation 21:1-4

Prayer: Lord Jesus, through my sharing of your Cross,
           take me today into your kingdom.

Then suddenly, while I was looking at the same crucifix as before, Jesus changed the appearance of his blessed face. The change of his blessed face changed mine also, and I felt glad and joyful to the highest degree possible. Then our Lord gently brought to my mind: "Where has all your pain and anguish gone to now?" And I was full of joy. I understood that for our Lord we are now with him on the Cross in our pains, and that in our suffering we are dying, and with his help and grace we willingly remain on the same Cross until the last moment. Then suddenly we shall see the expression of his face change, and then we shall be with him in heaven. Between one and the other there shall be no lapse of time; all shall be transformed into joy. This is what he meant when he said to me: "Where is all your pain and all your suffering now?" Thus we shall be full of happiness.

Here I saw truly that if he were to show us his blessed face now there would be no pain on earth, or in any other place, that could trouble us, but all would be joy and bliss for us. But because he shows his face of suffering while he carried his Cross in this life, therefore we suffer pain and turmoil with him, as our nature demands. And the reason why he suffered is that out of his goodness he wants to make us, with him, heirs of his joy. Moreover, as an exchange for the little pains we suffer in this life we shall have a sublime and eternal knowledge of God which we could never have otherwise. The harder our pains have been with him on the Cross, the greater will our glory be with him in his kingdom.

RDL ch. 21

The cross is the only ladder to heaven

The cross is the unique sacrifice of Christ, the "one mediator between God and men" (1 Tm 2:5). But because in his incarnate divine person he has in some way united himself to every man, the possibility of being made partners, in a way known to God, in the paschal mystery is offered to all men. He calls his disciples to "take up your cross and follow" him (Mt 16:24), for "Christ also suffered for us, leaving us an example so that we should follow in his steps" (1 Pt 2:21). In fact Jesus desires to associate with his redeeming sacrifice those who were to be its first beneficiaries (cf. Mk 10:39; Jn 21:18-19; Col 1:24). This is achieved supremely in the case of his mother, who was associated more intimately than any other person in the mystery of his redemptive suffering. "Apart from the cross there is no other ladder by which we may get to heaven."[3]

CCC 618

---

3. St. Rose of Lima, in P. Hansen, *Vita Mirabilis* (Louvain, 1668).

The Ninth Revelation

The Blessed Trinity

Then our good Lord Jesus Christ asked me: "Are you well satisfied that I suffered for you?" I said: "Yes, good Lord, and I thank you very much. Yes, good Lord, may you be blessed."

Then Jesus our good Lord said: "If you are satisfied, I am satisfied. To have ever suffered the Passion for you is for me a great joy, a bliss, an endless delight; and if I could suffer more I would do so."

RDL ch. 22

We Are His Joy, His Reward, His Glory, His Crown

Stricken with remorse, each will say to the other,
say with a groan and in distress of spirit:
"This is the man we used to laugh at once,
a butt for our sarcasm, fools that we were!
His life we regarded as madness,
his end as without honour.
How has he come to be counted as one of the sons of God?
How does he come to be assigned a place among the saints?"
But the virtuous live for ever,
their recompense lies with the Lord,
the Most High takes care of them.
So they shall receive the royal crown of splendour,
the diadem of beauty from the hand of the Lord;
for he will shelter them with his right hand
and shield them with his arm.

Wisdom 5:3-5; 16-17

Prayer: Heavenly Father, I thank you for gifting me to your Son, our Savior.

We belong to Jesus, not only because he has redeemed us, but also by the courteous gift of his Father. We are his joy, we are his reward, we are his glory, we are his crown. And that we are his crown is a singular marvel and a joyful sight!

What I was just saying is for Jesus such a great joy that he counts as nothing his tribulations, his Passion and his cruel and shameful death. And in these words, "If I could suffer more, I would do so," I saw truly that as often as he could die, he would die, and his love would never let him rest until he had done it. And I contemplated with great diligence to see how often he would have died if he could have. Truly, the number of the times went beyond my understanding and my intelligence so totally that my reason could not take it in.

And even if he had died or had wanted to die so many times, even then he would have counted that as nothing, out of love of us. Everything is so little compared to his great love. Indeed, although the sweet humanity of Christ can suffer only once, his goodness would never stop him offering himself. Every day he is ready to do the same again if that were possible.

The love which made him suffer surpasses all his pains as the heavens are above the earth, for that suffering was a noble, precious and glorious deed, accomplished once in time by the working of love. And that love was without beginning, and is and shall be without end. It was because of this love that he said so very sweetly, "If I could suffer more, I would suffer more". He did not say, "If it were necessary to suffer more," but "if I could suffer more," for even if it were not necessary, and he could suffer more, he would do it. This deed and work for our salvation was prepared by God with due excellence. In Christ I saw complete joy, for his joy would not have been complete if what has been done could have been done in a better way.

RDL ch. 22

Christ's sacrifice: a gift from the Father, an offering by the Son

The cup of the New Covenant, which Jesus antici-pated when he offered himself at the Last Supper, is afterwards accepted by him from his Father's hands in his agony in the garden at Gethsemane (cf. Mt 26:42; Lk 22:20), making himself "obedient unto death." Jesus prays: "My Father, if it is possible, let this cup pass from me . . ." (Phil 2:8; Mt 26:39; cf. Heb 5:7-8). Thus he expresses the horror that death represented for his human nature. Like ours, his human nature is destined for eternal life; but unlike ours, it is perfectly exempt from sin, the cause of death (cf. Rom 5:12; Heb 4:15). Above all, his human nature has been assumed by the divine person of the "Author of life," the "Living One" (cf. Acts 3:15; Rv 1:17; Jn 1:4; 5:26). By accepting in his human will that the Father's will be done, he accepts his death as redemptive, for "he himself bore our sins in his body on the tree" (1 Pt 2:24; cf. Mt 26:42).

CCC 612

This sacrifice of Christ is unique; it completes and surpasses all other sacrifices (cf. Heb 10:10). First, it is a gift from God the Father himself, for the Father handed his Son over to sinners in order to reconcile us with himself. At the same time it is the offering of the Son of God made man, who in freedom and love offered his life to his Father through the Holy Spirit in reparation for our disobedience (cf. Jn 10:17-18; 15:13; Heb 9:14; 1 Jn 4:10).

CCC 614

The Blessed Trinity Rejoices in Our Salvation

"Yahweh created me when his purpose first unfolded,
before the oldest of his works.
From everlasting I was firmly set,
from the beginning, before earth came into being.
When he fixed the heavens firm, I was there,
when he drew a ring on the surface of the deep,
when he thickened the clouds above,
when he fixed the springs of the deep,
when he assigned the sea its boundaries
— and the waters will not invade the shore –
when he laid down the foundations of the earth,
I was by his side, a master craftsman,
delighting him day after day, ever at play in his presence,
at play everywhere in his world,
delighting to be with the sons of men."

Proverbs 8:22-23, 27-31

Prayer: Most Holy Trinity, union of dearest Father,
           beloved Son, sweet Spirit, my joy and delight.

Oh Jesus, let us truly take notice of this bliss that the Blessed Trinity has in our salvation, and let us desire to have as much spiritual delight, with his grace. That is to say, that the delight in our salvation be like the joy which Christ has in our salvation, as far as that is possible while we are here on earth.

The whole Trinity was at work in the Passion of Christ, giving us an abundance of virtues and plenteous grace through him. But only the Maiden's Son suffered, for which the whole Blessed Trinity endlessly rejoices. This was shown in these words: "Are you well satisfied?" And by that other word which Christ said: "If you are well satisfied, I am well satisfied"; as if he said, "It is enough joy and delight to me, and I ask nothing else from you for my suffering except that I can well satisfy you."

In this he brought to my mind the quality of a glad giver. Every glad giver takes little notice of the thing that is given — all the desire and intention is to please and comfort the one to whom he gives the gift. And if the recipient accepts the gift gladly and thankfully, then the gracious giver counts as nothing all that was spent and suffered, for the joy and the delight that is had through pleasing and comforting the loved one. This was shown to me most fully and clearly.

RDL ch. 23

"In the name of the Father and of the Son and of the Holy Spirit"

The mystery of the Most Holy Trinity is the central mystery of Christian faith and life. It is the mystery of God in himself. It is therefore the source of all the other mysteries of faith, the light that enlightens them. It is the most fundamental and essential teaching in the hierarchy of the truths of faith. The whole history of salvation is identical with the history of the way and the means by which the one true God, Father, Son and Holy Spirit, reveals himself to men and reconciles and unites with himself those who turn away from sin.

CCC 234

The eternal origin of the Holy Spirit is revealed in his mission in time. The Spirit is sent to the apostles and to the Church both by the Father in the name of the Son, and by the Son in person, once he had returned to the Father (cf. Jn 14:26; 15:26; 16:14). The sending of the person of the Spirit after Jesus' glorification (cf. Jn 7:39) reveals in its fullness the mystery of the Holy Trinity.

CCC 244

The
Tenth
Revelation

The Depth of Christ's Love

With a glad expression our good Lord looked at his wounded side and contemplated it with joy and with his sweet gaze he led the understanding of this creature on through the same wound into his side, right inside it. And there he showed me a beautiful and enjoyable place, big enough to contain all humankind that shall be saved, that they might rest there in peace and in love. And with this he brought to my mind his priceless blood and the precious water which he had allowed to flow out for love of us. In this sweet contemplation he showed his blessed heart, cloven in two.

RDL ch. 24

My Dear One, Look and See Your Endless Joy

Take courage, Jerusalem:
he who gave you that name will console you.
Jerusalem, turn your eyes to the east,
see the joy that is coming to you from God.
Jerusalem, take off your dress of sorrow and distress,
put on the beauty of the glory of God for ever,
wrap the cloak of the integrity of God around you,
put the diadem of the glory of the Eternal on your head:
since God means to show your splendour
to every nation under heaven,
since the name God gives you for ever will be,
"Peace through integrity, and honour through devotedness."
Arise, Jerusalem, stand on the heights
and turn your eyes to the east:
see your sons reassembled from west and east
at the command of the Holy One,
jubilant that God has remembered them.

Baruch 4:30, 36; 5:1-5

Prayer: Jesus, my peace, my glory, my splendor,
let my heart tell you of my joy in you.

And with this our good Lord said most blissfully: "See how much I love you!" as if he had said, "My dear one, behold and see your Lord, your God, who is your Creator and your endless joy. See your own Brother, your Saviour. My child, behold and see what delight and bliss I have in your salvation, and for my love rejoice now with me."

And further, to help me understand more deeply, this blessed word was said: "See how much I love you!" It was as if he had said: "Behold and see that I loved you so much before I died for you that I was willing to die for you. Now I have died for you and suffered willingly what I could, and now all my bitter pain and all my hard turmoil has turned into endless joy and bliss for me and for you. How should it be that when you now ask me for anything that pleases me, that I should not give it to you with pleasure? For my pleasure is in your holiness, in your endless joy and bliss with me.

This has been shown to me by our good Lord in order to make us glad and happy.

RDL ch. 24

He knew and loved us all when he offered his life

The desire to embrace his Father's plan of redeeming love inspired Jesus' whole life (cf. Lk 12:50; 22:15; Mt 16:21-23), for his redemptive Passion was the very reason for his Incarnation. And so he asked, "And what shall I say? Father, save me from this hour? No, for this purpose I have come to this hour" (Jn 12:27). And again, "Shall I not drink the cup which the Father has given me?" (Jn 18:11). From the cross, just before "It is finished," he said, "I thirst" (Jn 19:30; 19:28).

CCC 607

It is love "to the end" (Jn 13:1) that confers on Christ's sacrifice its value as redemption and reparation, as atonement and satisfaction. He knew and loved us all when he offered his life (cf. Gal 2:20; Eph 5:2, 25). Now "the love of Christ controls us, because we are convinced that one has died for all; therefore all have died" (2 Cor 5:14). No man, not even the holiest, was ever able to take on himself the sins of all men and offer himself as a sacrifice for all. The existence in Christ of the divine person of the Son, who at once surpasses and embraces all human persons, and constitutes himself as the Head of all mankind, makes possible his redemptive sacrifice *for all*.

CCC 61

The Eleventh Revelation

Christ's Mother, Mary

With this same expression of mirth and joy, our good Lord looked down to his right side and brought to my mind where our Lady stood at the time of his Passion and he said: "Would you like to see her?" This sweet word sounded as if he had said: "I know quite well that you would like to see my blessed Mother, for after myself she is the highest joy that I could show you. She is the greatest pleasure and honour to me, and the one whom all my blessed creatures most desire to see."

RDL ch. 25

Rejoice with Me in My Love for Her

She is a breath of the power of God,
pure emanation of the glory of the Almighty;
hence nothing impure can find a way into her.
She is a reflection of the eternal light,
untarnished mirror of God's active power,
image of his goodness.

Wisdom 7:25-26

Prayer: Lord, may Mary, who understands what is pleasing to
           you, teach me and help me.

Because of the unique, exalted and wonderful love that he
has for this sweet maiden, his blessed Mother, our Lady
Saint Mary, he showed her bliss and her joy through this
sweet word, as if he said: "Would you like to see how I love
her, so that you can rejoice with me in the love I have for her
and she for me?" For after himself she is the most blissful
sight.[1]

But here I was not taught that I should long to see her
physical presence whilst I am here on earth, but rather to seek
the virtues of her blessed soul — her truth, her wisdom, her
love — through which I may know myself, and reverently
fear my God.

---

1. Referring to Mary as a *new Eve* ("so that just as a woman had a share in bringing
   about death, so also a woman should contribute to life"), the ecumenical church
   council Vatican II commented that "Mary has by grace been exalted above all
   angels and men *to a place second only to her Son*, as the most holy Mother of God." It
   then pointed out that the great honor, love and invocation given by Christians to
   the Blessed Virgin, from the earliest times through to our day, differs essentially
   from that worship, adoration and obedience given only to God; ". . . the duties
   and privileges of the Blessed Virgin . . . always refer to Christ, the source of all
   truth, sanctity and devotion," (Vatican II, *Lumen Gentium*, 1964).

Jesus showed me a spiritual sight of her. And just as I had seen her before, little and simple, so he showed her to me now, exalted, noble and glorious, more pleasing to him than all other creatures. He wants it to be known that all who take delight in him should take delight in her, and rejoice in the delight that he has in her and she in him.

To help us understand more clearly, he showed me this example: if a person loves another in a special way above all others, he will want everyone else to love and delight in that person whom he loves so much.

RDL ch. 25

The Holy Spirit will come upon you

The Annunciation to Mary inaugurates "the fullness of time" (Gal 4:4), the time of the fulfilment of God's promises and preparations. Mary was invited to conceive him in whom the "whole fullness of deity" would dwell "bodily" (Col 2:9). The divine response to her question, "How can this be, since I know not man?" was given by the power of the Spirit: "The Holy Spirit will come upon you" (Lk 1:34-35).

CCC 484

To become the mother of the Saviour, Mary was enriched by God with gifts appropriate to such a role. The angel Gabriel at the moment of the annunciation salutes her as "full of grace" (Lk 1:28). In fact, in order for Mary to be able to give the free assent of her faith to the announcement of her vocation, it was necessary that she be wholly borne by God's grace.

CCC 490

Through the centuries the Church has become ever more aware that Mary, "full of grace" (Lk 1:28) through God, was redeemed from the moment of her conception.

CCC 491

The splendour of an entirely unique holiness by which Mary is enriched from the first instant of her conception comes wholly from Christ: she is redeemed, in a more exalted fashion, by reason of the merits of her Son. The Father blessed Mary more than any other created person "in Christ with every spiritual blessing in the heavenly places" and chose her "in Christ before the foundation of the world, to be holy and blameless before him in love" (cf. Eph 1:3-4).

CCC 492

Jesus is Mary's only son, but her spiritual motherhood extends to all men whom indeed he came to save: the Son whom she brought forth is he whom God placed as the first-born among many brethren, that is, the faithful in whose generation and formation she co-operates with a mothers's love (cf. Jn 19:26-27; Rom 8:29; Rv 12:17).

CCC 501

The
Twelfth
Revelation

Christ Glorified

After this our Lord showed himself more glorified than I had ever seen him before.

By this I was taught that our soul will never have rest until it comes to him, knowing that he is the fullness of joy, homely and courteous, the fullness of bliss and true life itself.

RDL ch. 26

I Am the One, I Am the One

I pray not only for these,
but for those also
who through their words will believe in me.
May they all be one.
Father, may they be one in us,
as you are in me and I am in you,
so that the world may believe it was you who sent me.
I have given them the glory you gave to me,
that they may be one as we are one.
With me in them and you in me,
may they be so completely one
that the world will realise that it was you who sent me
and that I have loved them as much as you loved me.

John 17:20-23

Prayer: Lord, that in imitating you, I may be one with you
         and with all who love you.

Our Lord Jesus repeatedly said: "It is I, it is I. It is I who am the highest. It is I whom you love. It is I in whom you rejoice. It is I whom you serve. It is I for whom you long. It is I whom you desire. It is I whom you mean. It is I who am the all. It is I whom Holy Church preaches and teaches to you. It is I who showed himself to you before."

The number of words surpass my will and my understanding and all my powers. They were most sublime, for in them is comprehended what I am unable to tell. But the joy which I saw in that revelation surpasses all that the heart can wish, or the soul desire. Therefore these words cannot be explained here; but may everyone, according to the grace God gives to each in understanding and loving, receive them as intended by our Lord.

RDL ch. 26

Oneness with Christ

All Christ's riches are for every individual and are everybody's property. Christ did not live his life for himself but for us, from his incarnation "for us men and for our salvation" to his death "for our sins" and Resurrection "for our justification" (1 Cor 15:3; Rom 4:25). He is still "our advocate with the Father," who "always lives to make intercession" for us (1 Jn 2:1; Heb 7:25). He remains ever "in the presence of God on our behalf, bringing before him all that he lived and suffered for us" (Heb 9:24).

CCC 519

In all of his life Jesus presents himself as our model. He is the "perfect man" (cf. Rom 15:5; Phil 2:5), who invites us to become his disciples and follow him. In humbling himself, he has given us an example to imitate, through his prayers he draws us to pray, and by his poverty he calls us to accept freely the privations and persecutions that may come our way.

CCC 520

Christ enables us to live in him all that he himself lived, and he lives it in us. By his incarnation, he, the Son of God, has in a certain way united himself with each man. We are called only to become one with him, for he enables us as the members of his Body to share in what he lived for us in the flesh as our model.

CCC 521

The Thirteenth Revelation

The Weakness of Sin and the Power of God

After this the Lord brought to my mind the longing I had for him earlier, and I saw that nothing hindered me except sin.

This I saw to be generally true of us all. I thought to myself: "If there had been no sin, we should all have been pure and clean like our Lord, as he created us." In my foolishness, before this time, I had often wondered why God in his great foresight and wisdom did not prevent the beginning of sin in the first place. For then, I thought, all would be well.

This curious wondering would have been better left alone, but instead I mourned and sorrowed over it without reason or discretion. But Jesus, who in this vision instructed me about everything I needed to know, answered me with this word: "Sin is necessary, but all shall be well, and all shall be well, and all manner of things shall be well."

RDL ch. 27

All Shall Be Well, All Shall Be Well

Then fixing his eyes on his disciples he said:
"How happy are you who are poor:
yours is the kingdom of God.
Happy are you who are hungry now: you shall be satisfied.
Happy you who weep now: you shall laugh.
Rejoice when that day comes and dance for joy,
for then your reward will be great in heaven."

Luke 6:20-21, 23a

Prayer: Lord, may I be empty of self and poor; hungry for you;
            happy in weeping for my sin.

B y this bare word "sin," our Lord meant me to understand
in general all that is not good. It includes the shameful
contempt and uttermost tribulation that our Lord endured for
us in this life, his death with all his pains, and the suffering of
all his creatures both in the spirit and in the body. For all of us
are at times distressed and we shall continue to be so (like
Jesus our Master) until we are wholly purified in our mortal
flesh and in all our interior affections that are not wholly
good.

And in this sight with all the pains that ever were or ever
shall be, I understood the Passion of Christ to be the greatest
pain, far surpassing them all. All this was shown to me in an
instant of time and quickly passed over into comfort. For our
good Lord did not want the soul to be frightened by this ugly
sight. But sin itself I did not see, because I believe that sin does
not have its own substance or any form of being, nor can it be

known except through the pain it causes.[1] This pain is something very real and it lasts for a while, because it purifies us, makes us know ourselves, and ask for mercy. But the Passion of our Lord is a comfort to us in all this, and that is his blessed will. Because of the tender love that our Lord has for those who shall be saved, he gives comfort quickly and sweetly, saying, "Yes, it is true, sin is the root and cause of all pain, but all shall be well, and all manner of things shall be well."

When we shall know this mystery, then we shall truly know why God allowed sin to come, and knowing that we shall rejoice in him for ever.

RDL ch. 27

---

1. Julian states, "But sin itself I did not see" and explains that this is because sin has no substance or reality. God saw all that he had made and saw that it was very good (Gn 1:31) — all creation then reflects and mirrors his perfection and goodness. Through him all things came to be and without him nothing was made (Jn 1:3). Since only God has power to create, there can be no reality or substance outside his creation in which he is ever immanent and always acting. The summit of his creation is the human person, now enriched and dignified by God taking upon himself, in the Second Person of the Trinity, the body and nature of humanity. In Jesus is all the divine perfection of God, joined to human nature made perfect and therefore fully realised. In Jesus (with whom are always present the other two Persons of the Trinity, since the three are indivisibly one) is all reality — outside of him is no thing. Sin is a denial, a refusal, of the providence of God. Sin is the deprivation of goodness. Therefore sin is a choice of departure from God, and his care of us in the totality of his goodness, into nothingness. "Evil is not a substance," wrote Augustine. "The whole difficulty of understanding Hell is that the thing to be understood is so nearly Nothing," wrote C.S. Lewis. God made his creation *very good,* "so we must conclude that if things are deprived of all good, they cease altogether to be" (Augustine, *Confessions* VII:12). From all this, one can understand that evil and sin, being a choice (for we are given free will), "exist" only in the attitude taken to the good things God has given us, and can only be known through the pain it causes by the refusal of goodness. Sin is always known by its negativeness and destructiveness (for example, in violent discrimination against other persons, as in the holocaust against the Jewish People and as in acts of abortion, the killing of the unborn person) while goodness always positively builds and strengthens in order to bring all things to their perfection and full reality.

The inexhaustible source of forgiveness

It is precisely in the Passion, when the mercy of Christ is about to vanquish it, that sin most clearly manifests its violence and its many forms: unbelief, murderous hatred, shunning and mockery by the leaders and the people, Pilate's cowardice and the cruelty of the soldiers, Judas' betrayal — so bitter to Jesus, Peter's denial and the disciples' flight. However, at the very hour of darkness, the hour of the prince of this world (cf. Jn 14:30), the sacrifice of Christ secretly becomes the source from which the forgiveness of our sins will pour forth inexhaustibly.

CCC 1851

Our Compassion for Others Is Christ in Us

"Be compassionate as your Father is compassionate.
Do not judge, and you will not be judged yourselves;
do not condemn, and you will not be condemned yourselves;
grant pardon, and you will be pardoned.
Because the amount you measure out
is the amount you will be given back."

Luke 6:36-37, 38b

Prayer: Jesus, empty me of all judgement of others,
          and be my compassion to others.

Then I saw that every natural, loving feeling of compassion that anyone has for a fellow-Christian is due to Christ living within; and all the self-emptying which Christ revealed in his Passion was shown again in this compassion. In this there are two different kinds of understanding in our Lord's meaning; one is the bliss to which we shall be brought in which he wants us to rejoice, the other is the comfort for us in our pain. For he wants us to know it shall all be transformed into glory and profit by the power of his Passion, and to know that we do not suffer alone, but with him. He also wants us to see that he is our ground and that his pains and tribulations so far exceed all that we can suffer that it cannot be fully understood.

Taking good notice of this will prevent us from grumbling and despairing in our own sufferings. It makes us see truly that our sin deserves it, but his love excuses us. And in his great courtesy he does away with all our blame and looks upon us, with pity and compassion, as innocent and beloved children.

RDL ch. 28

Love one another as I have loved you

Jesus makes charity the new commandment (cf. Jn 13:34). By loving his own "to the end" (cf. Jn 13:1), he makes manifest the Father's love which he receives. By loving one another, the disciples imitate the love of Jesus which they themselves receive. Whence Jesus says: "As the Father has loved me, so I have loved you; abide in my love." And again: "This is my commandment, that you love one another as I have loved you" (Jn 15:9, 12).

CCC 1823

The practice of the moral life animated by charity gives to the Christian the spiritual freedom of the children of God.

CCC 1828

God Thirsts for Us

Jesus replied: "If you only knew what God is offering
and who it is that is saying to you:
Give me a drink,
you would have been the one to ask,
and he would have given you living water".

John 4:10

Prayer: Lord, in your thirsting for me, inspire my thirsting
and longing for you.

As our head, Christ is glorified and is incapable of
suffering, but in his body (in which all his members are
joined together) he is not yet fully glorified nor completely
beyond suffering. Therefore the same thirst and longing
which he experienced upon the Cross (that is, the desire,
longing and thirst which, as I see it, were in him from the very
beginning) he has them still, and will have them until the last
soul to be saved has come up into his bliss.

For as truly as there is in God the attribute of compassion
and pity, so truly is there in God the attribute of thirst and
longing. And by the power of this longing in Christ we in turn
must long for him: without which no soul comes to heaven.
This attribute of longing and thirst comes from the endless
goodness of God, just as pity does. And although he has both
longing and pity, these are two different attributes; from
them both together there arises his spiritual thirst, which
continues as long as we are in need, drawing us up into his
eternal bliss.

All this was revealed as a revelation of his compassion, for
it will cease on Judgement Day. So he has pity and compas-

sion for us and a longing to have us with him; but his wisdom and his love do not allow the end to come until the best time.

RDL ch. 31

God thirsts that we may thirst for him

"If you knew the gift of God!" (Jn 4:10). The wonder of prayer is revealed beside the well where we come seeking water: there, Christ comes to meet every human being. It is he who first seeks us and asks us for a drink. Jesus thirsts; his asking arises from the depths of God's desire for us. Whether we realise it or not, prayer is the encounter of God's thirst with ours. God thirsts that we may thirst for him.

CCC 2560

Be at Peace and Enjoy God

"But you, you must not set your hearts
on things to eat and things to drink;
nor must you worry.
No; set your hearts on his kingdom,
and these other things will be given you as well.
There is no need to be afraid, little flock,
for it has pleased your Father to give you the kingdom."
Luke 12:29, 31, 32

Prayer: Jesus, set your words in my heart so they be a bulwark against my worries.

Christ wants us to know that he takes care not only of the noble and great things but also of the humble and small, the lowly and simple things — all are equal. That is what he means when he says: "All manner of things shall be well." He wants us to know that even the least things will not be forgotten.

There is still one deed which the Blessed Trinity shall do on the last day, as I see it. But what the deed will be and how it will be done is unknown to all God's creatures that are below Christ. And this will be so until the deed is done. In goodness and love, our Lord God wants us to know that this deed will be done, but in his power and his wisdom he wants, through that same love, to conceal from us what it shall be and how it shall be done. The reason why he wants us to know about this deed is that he wants us to feel more comfortable, remain at peace in love, and to stop looking at all the worrying things that can hold us back from truly enjoying him.

This is the great deed, ordained by our Lord God from all eternity, treasured and hidden within his blessed breast, and known only to himself, through which he will make all things well.

RDL ch. 32

The heart is the place of decision between life or death

The heart is the dwelling place where I am, where I live; according to the Semitic or biblical expression, the heart is the place "to which I withdraw." The heart is our hidden centre, beyond the grasp of our reason and of others; only the Spirit of God can fathom the human heart and know it fully. The heart is the place of decision, deeper than our psychic drives. It is the place of truth, where we choose life or death. It is the place of encounter, because as image of God we live in relation: it is the place of covenant.

CCC 2563

Our Weakness in Sin,
God's Power in Miracles

The apostles said to the Lord,
"Increase our faith."
The Lord replied,
"Were your faith the size of a mustard seed
you could say to this mulberry tree,
'Be uprooted and planted in the sea,'
and it would obey you."

Luke 17:5-6

Prayer: My Lord and God, I believe — help me in my unbelief.

God gave me a special insight and teaching regarding the working and showing of miracles. He said, "It is known that in times past I have worked miracles, many of them most noble and marvellous, glorious and great; and what I have done in the past, I am still doing and shall continue to do in times to come."

We know that before miracles take place there is sorrow and anguish and trouble. These come so that we may know our own weakness and the harm we have fallen into through sin, in order to humble us and make us cry to God for help and grace. And after that come great miracles. These come from the supreme power, wisdom and goodness of God. They show his might and the joys of heaven (as far as that is possible in this passing life) in order to strengthen our faith and increase our hope, in love. Therefore it pleases God to be known and worshipped through miracles.

Then he indicated to me that he does not want us to be weighed down by the sorrows and storms which befall us, because it has always been like this before the coming of miracles.

RDL ch. 36

All things are possible to one who believes

Just as Jesus prays to the Father and gives thanks before receiving his gifts, so he teaches us filial boldness: "Whatever you ask in prayer, believe that you receive it, and you will" (Mk 11:24). Such is the power of prayer and of faith that does not doubt: "all things are possible to him who believes" (Mk 9:23; cf. Mt 21:22).

Jesus is saddened by the "lack of faith" of his own neighbours and the "little faith" of his own disciples (cf. Mk 6:6; Mt 8:26) as he is struck with admiration at the great faith of the Roman centurion and the Canaanite woman (cf. Mt 8:10; 15:28).

CCC 2610

The prayer of faith consists not only in saying "Lord, Lord," but in disposing the heart to do the will of the Father (cf. Mt 7:21).

CCC 2611

Peace and Love Are always Active

"Now you must repent
and turn to God,
so that your sins may be wiped out,
and so that the Lord may send the time of comfort.
Then he will send you the Christ he has predestined,
that is Jesus.
It was for you in the first place
that God raised up his servant
and sent him to bless you
by turning every one of you from your wicked ways."

Acts 3:19-20, 26

Prayer: Lord, mercifully heal my wounds of sin so they be signs
          and trophies of victory over sin.

By contrition we are made clean; by compassion we are made ready; by true longing for God we are made worthy. These are the three means, as I see it, by which all souls get to heaven; that is to say, those who on earth have been sinners and who are destined to be saved.

For every sinful soul must be healed by these medicines. Yet though the sinner is healed, his wounds are still seen by God — not as wounds but as signs of honour. So we see things upside-down; as we are punished here on earth with sorrow and penance, so we shall be rewarded in heaven by the courteous love of our Almighty God, who wishes that none who come there lose in any way the benefits gained from their struggles. For God regards sin as sorrow and pain for those who love him; out of love, to those he attributes no blame.

The reward we shall receive will not be small — it shall be great, glorious and honourable. And so all shame shall be turned into honour and joy. For our courteous Lord does not want that his servants despair because they fall so often and so grievously: for our falling does not stop him loving us. Peace and love are always alive and active within us, though we are not always in a state of peace and love.

RDL ch. 39

Penance and renewal on the way to holiness

Christ, holy, innocent and undefiled, knew nothing of sin, but came only to expiate the sins of the people. The Church, however, clasping sinners to her bosom, at once holy and always in need of purification, follows constantly the path of penance and renewal (Heb 2:17; 7:26; 2 Cor 5:21). All members of the Church, including her ministers, must acknowledge that they are sinners (cf. 1 Jn 1:8-10). In everyone, the weeds of sin will still be mixed with the good wheat of the Gospel until the end of time (cf. Mt 13:24-30). Hence the Church gathers sinners already caught up in Christ's salvation but still on the way to holiness.

CCC 827

The Fourteenth Revelation

Learning How To Pray

After this our Lord showed me teaching about prayer. In this Revelation I saw that the Lord had in mind two conditions: one is rightful prayer, and the other, absolute trust.

Yet often our trust is half-hearted, because we are not sure God hears us. This is because we think we are not good enough, and because we feel nothing at all; for often we are as barren and dry after our prayers as we were before. So when we are in such state of mind, our foolishness becomes the cause of our weakness in prayer. I have experienced this myself.

Our Lord brought all this suddenly to my mind and revealed these words to me: "I am the ground of your praying."

RDL ch. 41

I Am the Ground of Your Praying

If anyone acknowledges that Jesus is the Son of God,
God lives in him, and he in God.
We are quite confident that if we ask him for anything,
and it is in accordance with his will, he will hear us;
and, knowing that whatever we may ask, he hears us,
we know we have already been granted what we asked of him.
1 John 4:15; 5:14-15

Prayer: Loving Lord, may my prayers be love's beseeching
of Love's eternal intention.

Our Lord brought all this suddenly to my mind and revealed these words to me: "I am the ground of your praying. First, it is my will that you have something, then I make you want it, then I make you actually pray for it, and you do so. How then should you not get what you have been praying for?" So our Lord gave me tremendous encouragement, as can be seen in these words.

Where he says, "And you pray for it," he shows the very great pleasure this brings him and the eternal reward that he will give us for our beseeching. Where he says, "How then should you not get what you have been praying for?" he is talking of an impossible thing, for it is totally impossible that we should beseech him for mercy and grace and not have it! For our good Lord makes us pray to him for mercy and grace — for all the things that our good Lord makes us pray for, he himself has planned for us from eternity. So we can see that it is not our praying which causes God to be good and gracious to us, but his own goodness itself. This he showed truly in all those sweet words: "I am the ground."

Our good Lord wills that all those who love him here on earth should know this. And if we use our commonsense, the more we grasp this, the more we shall pray — and this is what our Lord intends.

RDL ch. 41

Prayer as communion with Christ

In the New Covenant, prayer is the living relationship of the children of God with their Father who is good beyond all measure, with his Son Jesus Christ and with the Holy Spirit. The grace of the Kingdom is the union of the entire holy and royal Trinity with the whole human spirit. Thus, the life of prayer is the habit of being in the presence of the thrice-holy God and in communion with him. This communion of life is always possible because, through Baptism, we have already been united with Christ (cf. Rom 6:5). Prayer is *Christian* insofar as it is communion with Christ and extends throughout the Church, which is his Body. Its dimensions are those of Christ's love (cf. Eph 3:18-21).

CCC 2565

Enjoy Him in Happy Thanksgiving

You were darkness once,
but now you are light in the Lord;
be like children of light,
for the effects of the light are seen in complete goodness
and right living and truth.
Sing the words and tunes of the psalms and hymns
when you are together, and go on singing and chanting
to the Lord in your hearts,
so that always and everywhere you are giving thanks to God
who is our Father in the name of our Lord Jesus Christ.

Ephesians 5:8-9, 19-20

Prayer: Abba Father, I thank you for having heard me;
I know you always hear me.

Our Lord is very happy and glad with our prayer. He expects it and he wants to have it, because with his grace it makes us as like him in the way we feel as we are like him in our nature. Therefore this is his blessed will, for he says, "Pray wholeheartedly, even when you don't feel like it, for it is a very profitable thing to do, even if you don't feel that way. Pray wholeheartedly, even when you feel nothing, and see nothing, yes, even when you think you cannot do it. For in times of dryness and barrenness, in times of sickness and weakness, your prayer is most pleasing to me, though you may find it rather tasteless. And this holds good in my eyes for all your prayer said in faith."

Thanksgiving is also an integral part of prayer. Thanksgiving is a true inward awareness; with deep reverence and loving fear it leads us to turn with all our strength to the work the Lord is calling us to do, all the time rejoicing and thanking him in our hearts. Sometimes the soul is so full that it overflows into words and cries out: "Good Lord, thanks be to you, may you be blessed." Sometimes, when the heart is dry and feels nothing, or when the enemy is attacking, then reason and grace drive us to cry aloud to our Lord, recalling his holy Passion and his great goodness. Then the power of our Lord's word enters the soul, enlivens the heart, and leads it by his grace into true work for him, causing it to pray with utter happiness. To truly delight in our Lord is, for him, a most loving thanksgiving.

RDL ch. 41

The Giver is more precious than the gift

The evangelists have preserved two explicit prayers offered by Christ during his public ministry. Each begins with thanksgiving. The prayer before the raising of Lazarus is recorded by John (cf. Jn 11:41-42). Thanksgiving precedes the event: "Father, I thank you for having heard me," which implies that the Father always hears his petitions. Jesus immediately adds: "I know that you always hear me," which implies that Jesus, on his part, *constantly made such petitions.* Jesus' prayer, characterised by thanksgiving, reveals to us how to ask: *before* the gift is given, Jesus commits himself to the One who in giving gives himself. The Giver is more precious than the gift; he is the "treasure"; in him abides his Son's heart; the gift is given "as well" (Mt 6:21, 33).

CCC 2603-2604

Mercy and Grace Are Given before We Ask

Since in Jesus, the Son of God,
we have the supreme high priest
who has gone through to the highest heaven,
we must never let go of the faith that we have professed.
Let us be confident, then,
in approaching the throne of grace,
that we shall have mercy from him and find grace
when we are in need of help.

Hebrews 4:14, 16

Prayer: Lord Jesus, be the ground, the trust and faith,
and the fruit and goal of my prayer.

Our Lord wants us to have a correct understanding with regard to three things about prayer.

The first is, from whom and how our prayer originates. *From whom* he reveals when he says: "I am the ground," and *how* is by his goodness for he says, "First it is my will."

The second is, how we should use our prayers. The answer is that our will should merge joyfully into the will of our Lord. This is what he means when he says: "l will make you to want it."

The third concerns the fruit and the goal of our prayers, which is to be one with, and like to, our Lord in all things. For this intention and for this end was all this loving lesson shown. And he wishes to help us, and he will do so, as he said himself. Blessed may he be!

For it is our Lord's will that our prayer and our trust be both equally great. If our trust is not as great as our praying, then we are not fully honouring our Lord in our prayer. Further, we hinder and harm ourselves. The reason for this is,

I believe, that we do not truly know that our Lord is the ground from whom our prayer springs forth, and that it is given by grace out of his love. If we knew this we would surely be inspired to trust that our Lord will gift us with all that we desire. I am quite sure that no one ever asks for mercy and grace with right intentions unless mercy and grace have been given first.

RDL ch. 42

Prayer in trust and faith
bears the fruit of love and union

When Jesus openly entrusts to his disciples the mystery of prayer to the Father he reveals to them what their prayer and ours must be, once he has returned to the Father in his glorified humanity. What is new is to "ask *in his name*" (Jn 14:13). Faith in the Son introduces the disciples into the knowledge of the Father, because Jesus is "the way, and the truth, and the life" (Jn 14:6). Faith bears its fruit in love: it means keeping the word and the commandments of Jesus, it means abiding with him in the Father who, in him, so loves us that he abides with us. In this new covenant the certitude that our petitions will be heard is founded on the prayer of Jesus (cf. Jn 14:13-14).

CCC 2614

Prayer Unites the Soul to God

We pray continually that our God
will make you worthy of his call,
and by his power fulfil all your desires for goodness
and complete all that you have been doing through faith;
because in this way the name of our Lord Jesus Christ
will be glorified in you and you in him,
by the grace of our God and the Lord Jesus Christ.
                                            2 Thessalonians 1:11-12

Prayer: Jesus, Master of prayer, teach me and help me pray
          as you wish *me* to do.

Prayer unites the soul to God. For although, when restored
by grace, the soul is always like God in nature and in
substance, it is often unlike God in condition because of sin on
our part. Then prayer shows that the soul wills what God
wills, and it comforts the conscience and enables us to receive
grace. So God teaches us to pray, and mightily to trust that we
shall receive what we pray for; because he looks at us in love
and wants to make us his partners in his good will and work.
He therefore moves us to pray for what it pleases him to do. In
return for this prayer and good will, which are his gifts to us,
he will give us an eternal reward.

This was shown to me in his words: "And you pray for it."
In this word God showed such great pleasure and delight as if
he were in our great debt for all the good we do, when in fact it
is he who does it all. For this we beseech him fervently to do
whatever seems good to him. It is as if he said: "How could
you please me more than by beseeching me fervently, wisely
and earnestly to do what I shall do?" So the soul, by prayer, is
made one with God.

                                                    RDL ch. 43

The harmony of prayer
within a communion of love

Even more, what the Father gives us when our prayer is united with that of Jesus is "another Counsellor, to be with you for ever, the Spirit of truth" (Jn 14:16-17). This new dimension of prayer and of its circumstances is displayed throughout the farewell discourse (cf. Jn 14:23-26; 15:7,16; 16:13-15, 23-27). In the Holy Spirit, Christian prayer is a communion of love with the Father, not only through Christ but also *in him*: "Hitherto you have asked nothing in my name; ask, and you will receive, that your joy may be full" (Jn 16:24).

CCC 2615

Longing for His Love

"Do not let your hearts be troubled.
Trust in God still, and trust in me.
There are many rooms in my Father's house;
if there were not, I should have told you.
I am going now to prepare a place for you,
and after I have gone and prepared you a place,
I shall return to take you with me;
so that where I am you may be too."

John 14:1-3

Prayer: My Jesus, fill me with a trusting longing for you
           so that I may be where you are.

Thus in our own humble and constant prayer we shall, by his sweet grace, come to him now in this life by means of many intimate touches which bring sweet spiritual insight and experiences, measured out to us in so far as our simple natures can bear. All this is done and shall be done by the grace of the Holy Spirit, until we die, filled with longing for his love. Then we shall all come to our Lord, clearly knowing ourselves and fully possessing God. Then we shall be eternally hidden in God, truly seeing him and wholly touching him, spiritually hearing him, deliciously smelling him and tasting his sweetness!

Then we shall see God face to face, homely and wholly. The creature who is made will see and endlessly behold God who is the Maker. For no one can see God in this way and continue to live in this mortal life. But when God, by his special grace, wishes to reveal himself in this life, he raises his creature beyond its natural strength, and apportions the revelation according to his will and in the most beneficial way.

RDL ch. 43

In persevering prayer give humble, trusting, persevering love

"Pray constantly," "always and for everything giving thanks in the name of our Lord Jesus Christ to God the Father" (1 Thes 5:17; Eph 5:20). Paul adds, "Pray at all times in the Spirit, with all prayer and supplication. To that end keep alert with all perseverance making supplication for all the saints" (Eph 6:18). Against our dullness and laziness, the battle of prayer is that of humble, trusting and persevering *love*. This love opens our hearts to three enlightening and life-giving facts of faith about prayer.

It is always possible to pray . . .

Our time is in the hands of God: "It is possible to offer fervent prayer even while walking in public or strolling alone, or seated in your shop . . . while buying or selling . . . or even while cooking."[1]

Prayer is a vital necessity . . .

How can the Holy Spirit be our life if our heart is far from him?

Prayer and Christian life are inseparable . . .

"Whatever you ask the Father in my name, he [will] give it to you. This I command you, to love one another" (Jn 15:16-17).

CCC, from 2742-2745

---

1. This quotation, on the possibility of constant prayer wherever one is, comes from John Chrysostom (347-407), Bishop of Constantinople, known as one of the Four Greek Doctors of the Church. He is greatly loved and widely read in the Orthodox Church, and his teaching on constant, continual prayer is realized in the Orthodox tradition and practice of the invocation of the Holy Name, in the Scripture-based Jesus Prayer — "Lord Jesus Christ, Son of God, have mercy upon me, a sinner." This can be shortened to a single aspiration — "Jesus." The *Catechism of the Catholic Church* explains: "When the holy Name is repeated often by a humbly attentive heart, the prayer is not lost by heaping up empty phrases, but holds fast to the Word and brings forth fruit with patience. This prayer is possible at all times . . . (CCC 2668). A short, excellent and ecumenically-minded book on the practice in everyday life of this heart-centered prayer is *The Jesus Prayer*, by Per-Olof Sjögren, published by Triangle, SPCK, revised edition 1996. For readers unacquainted with the *Jesus Prayer* it will open up refreshing horizons in their prayer battle. "No matter where we happen to be, by prayer we can set up an altar to God in our heart" (John Chrysostom).

About
Certain Things
in the Previous
Fourteen Revelations

A Treasury of Faith

In all these Revelations God often showed me that we are evermore working according to God's will and for his glory, continually, without ceasing.

What this working is was shown in the first revelation in a wonderful way, for it was shown in the working of truth and wisdom in the soul of our blessed Lady, Saint Mary. I hope that, by the grace of the Holy Spirit, I shall be able to relate the matter as I have seen it.

RDL ch. 44

We Are Given God-Like Qualities

In making these gifts, he has given us the guarantee
of something very great and wonderful to come:
through them you will be able to share the divine nature,
and to escape corruption in a world that is sunk in vice.
But to attain this, you will have to do the utmost yourselves,
adding goodness to the faith that you have,
understanding to your goodness,
self-control to your understanding,
patience to your self-control,
true devotion to your patience,
kindness towards your fellow men to your devotion,
and, to this kindness, love.

2 Peter 1:4-7

Prayer: Lord, guide me by your kind judgements;
           teach me to leave all judgement to your mercy.

Truth sees God and Wisdom beholds God. From these two comes a third: that is a holy, marvelling delight in God, which is love. Where there is truth and wisdom there is truly love, truly coming from them both; and all are of God's making. For God is endless sovereign truth, endless sovereign wisdom and endless sovereign love. God, himself uncreated, has himself created us, giving our souls god-like qualities. The soul always does what it is created for: it sees God, beholds God, and loves God. God therefore rejoices in his creature, and the creature rejoices in God in endless wonder. In this wondering he sees his God, his Lord, his Creator so sublime, so great, so good that in comparison the creature seems hardly anything at all. But the brightness and clearness of truth and wisdom make him see and know that he is made for love, and in this love God keeps him for ever.

God bases his judgement of us on our essential nature, our true self, which in him is always kept whole and safe;[1] this judgement comes from his righteousness. But human judgement is based on our changeable, sensual nature which goes now one way, now in another, variably influenced by our higher or lower selves. Our human verdict is muddled; sometimes it is good and understanding, sometimes it is harsh and distressing. In so far as it is good it reflects and belongs to God's justice; where it is harsh and distressing our good Lord Jesus corrects it by his mercy and grace through the power of his blessed Passion, and conforms it with his rightful justice.

RDL ch. 45

---

1. "God bases his judgement of us on our essential nature." Julian has already stated that God has created man, giving his soul god-like qualities. Our essential nature, our true realization, is therefore in the image and likeness of God. Christians have been somewhat shy of following such statements through to their logical conclusion, perhaps for fear of the presumption shown by Adam — but he fell to the temptation of the enemy to seek to rival God and to obtain his own knowledge of good and evil independently of God. In contrast, Scripture and the Tradition of the Church teach us that God is love, and that accordingly he desires to share with us *all that he is* — "I pray not only for these, but those also who through their words will believe in me. May they all be one. *Father, may they be one in us . . .* " (Jn 17:20-21). The implication is radical but nevertheless clear and fundamental. Jesus, God made true and perfect man, prays that imperfect man may be "oned" with God, recreated in the divine perfections. God became man *to make us "partakers of the divine nature"* (2 Pt 1:4). "For the Son of God became man so that we might become God," Athanasius wrote. No wonder Peter, in his proclamation of this radical truth, pointed out that "to attain this, you will have to do the utmost yourselves"; though in truth we can do nothing of ourselves, but Christ does all for us. But we must desire to give our total and committed consent, and make ourselves fully open to Christ's action. A final point, in this brief summary, is that in our intended deified oneness with God in a total sharing in love, we (made in the image and likeness of the Blessed Trinity — Gn 1:26) retain our humanity in the diversity in unity of the community of love which is the Trinity. We become fully human and alive in our life in Christ. In him "lives the fullness of divinity, and in him you too find your own fulfilment" (Col 2:9).

He was made like us,
that we may be made like him

The Word became flesh to be our model of holiness: "Take my yoke upon you, and learn from me." "I am the way, and the truth, and the life; no one comes to the Father, but by me" (Mt 11:29; Jn 14:6).

CCC 459

The Word became flesh to make us "partakers of the divine nature" (2 Pt 1:4): "For this is why the Word became man, and the Son of God became the Son of man: so that man, by entering into communion with the Word and thus receiving divine sonship, might become a son of God."[2] "For the Son of God became man so that we might become God."[3] "The only-begotten Son of God, wanting to make us sharers in his divinity, assumed our nature, so that he, made man, might make men gods."[4]

CCC 460

2. Irenaeus, *Adversus haereses.*
3. Athanasius, *De incarnatione.*
4. Thomas Aquinas, *Opusculum.*

God Is Never Angry

For the sake of my name I deferred my anger,
for the sake of my honour I curbed it;
I did not destroy you.
And now I have put you in the fire like silver,
I have tested you in the furnace of distress.
Thus says Yahweh, your redeemer, the Holy One of Israel:
I, Yahweh, your God, teach you what is good for you,
I lead you in the way you must go.

Isaiah 48:9-10, 17

Prayer:　Lord of Mercy and Love, open my heart to you
as your heart was opened for me.

In this whole vision it seemed to me that it was necessary to accept and know that we are sinners, that we do many evil things which we ought not to do and leave many good deeds undone that we ought to do. So we deserve pain, blame and wrath. Yet in spite of all this, I saw truly that our Lord is never angry nor ever will be. Because he is God, he is goodness, he is truth, he is love and he is peace; and his power, his wisdom, his unity and his love do not allow him to be angry. For I truly saw that anger is contrary to his power, wisdom and goodness. God is the goodness that cannot be angry, for God is nothing but goodness. Our soul is knitted to him who is unchangeable goodness, and between God and our soul is neither anger nor the necessity for forgiveness, as he sees it. For our soul is so wholly knitted to God through his goodness that there can be nothing at all between God and our soul.

I saw no wrath except on our part, and that God forgives in us. Such wrath is a perverse opposition to peace and love. It comes either from our lack of power or lack of wisdom or lack of goodness — and that lack is not to be found in God, but in us. For we, because of sin and wretchedness, have within us an anger persistently opposed to peace and love. Our Lord often revealed this in his loving expression of compassion and pity. For the ground of mercy is love, and the work of mercy is to keep us safe in love. This was shown to me in such a way that I could not perceive mercy in any other way than in its complete unity with love.

RDL ch. 46; ch 48

Our response to this outpouring of mercy into our hearts

Now — and this is daunting — this outpouring of mercy cannot penetrate our hearts as long as we have not forgiven those who have trespassed against us. Love, like the Body of Christ, is indivisible; we cannot love the God we cannot see if we do not love the brother or sister we do see (cf. 1 Jn 4:20). In refusing to forgive our brothers and sisters, our hearts are closed and their hardness makes them impervious to the Father's merciful love; but in confessing our sins, our hearts are opened to his grace.

CCC 2840

Our Anger Is Dispelled by Mercy and Forgiveness

I have dispelled your faults like a cloud,
your sins like a mist.
Come back to me,
for I have redeemed you.
Thus says Yahweh, your redeemer,
he who formed you in the womb.

Isaiah 44:22, 24a

Prayer: Jesus, calm and dispel my tensions and inner anger
in the depths of your peace.

I saw with absolute certainty that just as on the one hand our perversity produces pain, shame and sorrow in us while here on earth, so on the other hand in heaven grace produces consolation, praise and bliss so much more abundantly for us; so that when we come up there and receive the sweet reward that grace has won for us, we shall thank and bless our Lord, endlessly rejoicing ever to have endured suffering. That shall be because of a property of the blessed love which we shall know in God and which we might never have known without first suffering. When I saw all this, I was forced to agree that the mercy and forgiveness of God abate and dispel our wrath.

And so to the soul who by God's special grace is enabled to penetrate so far into the sublime and wonderful goodness of God, and to see that we are eternally united to him in love, it is the most impossible thing that God should be angry. Anger and friendship are two opposites. We must admit that God, who dispels and quenches our anger, and so makes us humble and gentle, must himself always be loving, humble and gentle. And this is the opposite of anger.

RDL ch. 48; ch 49

Trials are necessary
and are different from temptation

The Holy Spirit makes us discern between trials, which are necessary for the growth of the inner man (cf. Lk 8:13-15; Acts 14:22; Rom 5:3-5; 2 Tm 3:12), and temptation, which leads to sin and death (cf. Jas 1:14-15). We must also discern between being tempted, and consenting to temptation. Finally, discernment unmasks the lie of temptation, whose object appears to be good, a "delight to the eyes" (cf. Gn 3:6) and desirable, when in reality its fruit is death.

CCC 2847

By the Spirit Made
Christ's Gifted Children

So you are no longer aliens or foreign visitors;
you are citizens like all the saints,
and part of God's household.
You are part of a building
that has the apostles and prophets for its foundations,
and Christ Jesus himself for its main cornerstone.
As every structure is aligned on him,
all grow into one holy temple in the Lord;
and you too, in him, are being built into a house
where God lives, in the Spirit.

Ephesians 2:19-22

Prayer: Spirit of all fruitful gifts, build in me your life, to be Jesus' love to others.

Because of the great, eternal love that God has for all humankind, he makes no distinction in love between the blessed soul of Christ and the least soul that shall be saved. It is very easy to believe and to trust that the blessed soul of Christ has a place of honour within the glorious Godhead. But it is also true, as I have understood from what our Lord has shown me, that where the blessed soul of Christ is, there too is the essence of all the souls that shall be saved by him.

How greatly we should rejoice that God indwells in our soul! Yet how much more we rejoice that our soul dwells in God! Our soul has been created to be God's dwelling-place; and the soul's dwelling-place is God, who is uncreated. It is a great, inwardly illuminating understanding to have assurance that God, our Creator, dwells in our soul. Yet it is an even greater understanding to know that our soul, which is created, dwells in the essence, the very being of God! We are what we are because we come from that being.

I saw no difference between God and our essential being: all seemed to be God.

For Christ is mercifully at work in us, and we by means of grace yield ourselves to him through the gifts and the power of the Holy Spirit. This work in us enables us to be Christ's children and to live Christian lives.

RDL ch. 54

The Holy Spirit renews and strengthens us as children of light

"Justified in the name of the Lord Jesus Christ and in the Spirit of our God" (1 Cor 6:11), "sanctified . . . [and] called to be saints" (1 Cor 1:2), Christians have become the temple of the Holy Spirit (cf. 1 Cor 6:19). This "spirit of the Son" teaches them to pray to the

Father (cf. Gal 4:6) and, having become their life, prompts them to act so as to bear "the fruit of the Spirit" (Gal 5:22, 25) by charity in action. Healing the wounds of sin, the Holy Spirit renews us interiorly through a spiritual transformation (cf. Eph 4:23). He enlightens and strengthens us to live as "children of light" through "all that is good and right and true" (Eph 5:8, 9).

CCC 1695

Faith Grounded in Love, Reason and Purpose

He has let us know the mystery of his purpose,
the hidden plan he so kindly made in Christ from the beginning
to act upon when the times had run their course to the end;
that he would bring everything together under Christ, as head,
everything in the heavens and everything on earth.
May the God of our Lord Jesus Christ, the Father of glory,
give you a spirit of wisdom and perception of what is revealed,
to bring you to full knowledge of him.

Ephesians 1;9-10, 17

Prayer: Lord, I bless and praise you that you have enabled me to freely choose you.

Our faith comes from the natural love of our soul, from the clear light of our reason, and from the steadfast memory we have of God from the very first moment of our creation. When our soul is breathed into our body, giving life to our senses, then immediately mercy and grace begin to work, caring for us and protecting us with pity and love. At the same time the Holy Spirit forms in our faith the hope that, when we have grown in the fulfilment which comes to us from the Holy Spirit, we shall return to our essential being above, in the power of Christ. In this way I understood that our physical nature is founded in God's nature, mercy, and grace. This foundation enables us to receive gifts that lead us on to eternal life. For I saw with absolute certainty that our being is in God. I also saw that God is in our physical nature, because in the very same instance in which our soul is put into our physical being, it becomes the city of God. He comes into this city and will never depart from it again, for God is never out of the soul, but dwells in it blessedly without end.

This was said in the sixteenth Revelation where it says: "Jesus will never leave the place he occupies in our soul." All the gifts for us that God can give to his Son, Jesus, are given on our behalf. Living in us, Jesus holds these gifts within himself until we are fully grown in both body and soul — each helping the other — until we have reached perfect maturity by the process of nature. Then the Holy Spirit works in mercy in the depths of our nature, in his grace breathing into us gifts that lead to eternal life.

RDL ch. 55

We are rational and therefore like God

God created man a rational being, conferring on him the dignity of a person who can initiate and control his own actions. God willed that man should be "left in the hand of his own counsel" (Eccl 15:14),[5] so that he might of his own accord seek his Creator and freely

_____

5. The Jerusalem Bible translates it as: "left him free to make his own decisions."

attain his full and blessed perfection by cleaving to him. Man is rational and therefore like God; he is created with free will and is master over his acts.

CCC 1730

Freedom is the power, rooted in reason and will, to act or not to act, to do this or that, and so to perform deliberate actions on one's own responsibility. By free will one shapes one's own life. Human freedom is a force for growth and maturity in truth and goodness; it attains its perfection when directed toward God, our beatitude.

CCC 1731

The Blessings of God's Commandments

"Listen to instruction and learn to be wise,
do not ignore it.
Happy those who keep my ways!
Happy the man who listens to me,
who day after day watches at my gates
to guard the portals.
For the man who finds me finds life,
he will win favour from Yahweh;
but he who does injury to me does hurt to his own soul,
all who hate me are in love with death."

Proverbs 8:33-36

Prayer: Holy Spirit of mercy and grace, teach me
to faithfully attend, listen and learn.

The next good which we receive is our faith, which marks the beginning of further benefits. Faith flows from the great riches of our essential being into our sensual nature. It is grounded in us, and we in it, through the natural goodness of God by the working of mercy and grace. From this faith stem all the other good blessings by which we are led and saved. From faith come all the commandments of God, to be loved and kept. We ought to understand two aspects of God's commandments; first, there are his precepts which we should love and obey and, second, his prohibitions. We should know the things which God forbids, hating and rejecting them. All our activity for God is contained in these two aspects.

Also included in our faith are the seven sacraments,[6] each following the other in the order which God has ordained for us, and every kind of virtue. Those same virtues, which we have received from our essential being, given to us naturally in the goodness of God, are also given and renewed in us by the Holy Spirit working in mercy and grace. These virtues and gifts are kept as treasures for us in Jesus Christ. He wants us to be helpers in this work, to give him all our attention, learn his lessons, keep his laws, desire to do all as he does, and truly trust him.

RDL ch. 57

Attending and listening to conscience

By his reason, man recognises the voice of God which urges him to do what is good and avoid what is evil. Everyone is obliged to follow this law, which makes

---

6. The sacraments are seven in number and are the visible outward signs of effective inward divine action to build up the Body of Christ in holiness. They are — baptism, confirmation, the eucharist (holy communion), marriage, the pardoning of sins and reconciliation in penance, the healing anointing of the sick, and the ordaining of ministers in holy orders.

itself heard in conscience and is fulfilled in the love of God and of neighbour. Living a moral life bears witness to the dignity of the person.

CCC 1706

By his Passion, Christ delivered us from Satan and from sin. He merited for us the new life in the Holy Spirit. His grace restores what sin had damaged in us.

CCC 1708

The Trinity Is Our Father, Our Mother, Our Lord

Am I to open the womb and not bring to birth?
says Yahweh.
Or I, who bring to birth, am I to close it?
says your God.
Rejoice, Jerusalem,
be glad for her, all you who love her!
Rejoice, rejoice for her,
all you who mourned her!
That you may be suckled, filled,
from her consoling breast,
that you may savour with delight
her glorious breasts.

Isaiah 66:9-11

Prayer: Blessed Trinity, may your infinite perfections
be mirrored in all your children.

In our creation God Almighty is the Father of our human nature, God All-Wisdom is the Mother of our human nature; and with them is the love and goodness of the Holy

Spirit. And these are all one God, one Lord. In our one-ing with God, he is our very true husband and we his beloved wife, his lovely bride, with whom he is never displeased. For he says: "I love you and you love me, and our love shall never be sundered."

I contemplated the working of the Blessed Trinity, and I saw and I understood that there are three qualities in the one God: Fatherhood, Motherhood, and Lordship. Our essential being (ours since our creation before the beginning of time) is protected and kept in bliss by God the Father Almighty. In the Second Person of the Blessed Trinity, by his knowledge and wisdom, our physical nature is kept safe, restored and saved, for he is our Mother, our Father and our Saviour. And in our good Lord the Holy Spirit, we have our reward and recompense for our life of toil; and in this he infinitely surpasses, in his marvellous courtesy and in his most generous grace, all we could ever desire.

For all our life consists of three things: in the first we have our being, in the second we have our increasing, and in the third we have our fulfilment. The first is nature, the second is mercy, and the third is grace. In the first I saw and understood that the high power of the Trinity is our Father, the deep wisdom of the Trinity is our Mother and the great love of the Trinity is our Lord.

RDL ch. 58

We reflect the perfection of God

In no way is God in man's image. He is neither man nor woman. God is pure spirit in which there is no place for the differences between the sexes. But the respective "perfections" of man and woman reflect something of the infinite perfection of God: those of a mother and those of a father and husband (cf. Is 49:14-15; 66:13; Ps 131:2-3; Hos 11:1-4; Jer 3:4-19).

CCC 370

God Is as Truly Our Mother as Our Father

For thus says Yahweh:
Now towards her I send flowing peace,
like a river, and like a stream in spate,
the glory of the nations.
At her breast will her nurslings be carried
and fondled in her lap.
Like a son comforted by his mother
will I comfort you.

Isaiah 66:12-13a

Prayer: Yahweh, HE WHO IS, I thank you and praise you
for my creation, from nothing, in your love.

God is as truly our Mother as he is our Father. He revealed this in all the revelations, but especially in these sweet words, where he says: "I am the one." That is to say, "It is I — the power, and goodness of fatherhood; It is I — the wisdom of motherhood; It is I — the light and grace of blessed love, the Trinity; It is I — the unity; It is I — the supreme goodness of every kind of thing; It is I — who enable you to love, to long; It is I — the endless fulfilling of all true desires."

For the soul is highest, noblest and worthiest when it is lowliest, humblest and gentlest. It is from our essential ground in God that we receive as natural gifts all the virtues of our physical natures, helped and furthered by mercy and grace, without which we can make no progress. Our great Father, Almighty God, who is Being, knows and loves us from before time began. In this knowledge, out of his wonderful deep love, and with the eternal foreseeing and consent of the Blessed Trinity, he willed that the Second Person should become our Mother, our Brother and our Saviour. From this it follows that as truly as God is our Father, so truly is God our Mother.

Our Father wills it, our Mother accomplishes it, our good Lord the Holy Spirit confirms it. So we must love our God in whom we have our being. We must reverently thank and praise him for creating us, fervently praying to our Mother for mercy and compassion, and to our Lord the Holy Spirit for help and grace. For in these three is all our life: nature, mercy and grace. From these we have gentleness, patience, pity, and hatred of sin and wickedness, for it is in the nature of virtue to hate sin and wickedness.

So Jesus is our true Mother in nature through creating us in the first place, and he is our true Mother in grace through taking on himself our created nature. All the loving service and all the sweet and gentle care of precious motherhood are in the Second Person, for in him our will for God is whole and safe for ever, both in nature and in grace, by of his own innate goodness.

RDL ch. 59

I am the one — HE WHO IS

The revelation of the ineffable name "I AM WHO AM" contains the truth that God alone IS. . . . God is the fullness of Being and of every perfection, without origin and without end. All creatures receive all that they are and have from him; but he alone is his very being, and he is of himself everything that he is.

CCC 213

God, "HE WHO IS," revealed himself to Israel as the one "abounding in steadfast love and faithfulness" (Ex 34:6). These two terms express summarily the riches of the divine name. In all his works God displays not only his kindness, goodness, grace and steadfast love, but also his trustworthiness, constancy, faithfulness and truth.

CCC 214

Our Mother Jesus Feeds Us in the Sacraments

"Approach me, you who desire me,
and take your fill of my fruits,
for memories of me are sweeter than honey,
inheriting me is sweeter than the honeycomb.
They who eat me will hunger for more,
they who drink me will thirst for more.
Whoever listens to me will never have to blush,
whoever acts as I dictate will never sin."

Ecclesiasticus 24:19-22

Prayer: Jesus, joy of our desiring, bread of angels, wine of redemption, I adore you.

Our Mother in nature (who is also our Mother in grace because he wanted to become our Mother in all things) began his work in complete humility and gentleness, in the

Virgin's womb. In this humble place our great God, the supreme wisdom of all things, arrayed himself in our poor flesh, and fully prepared himself to do the work and service of motherhood in all things.

The service of the mother is nearest, readiest and most reliable. Its nearness is because it is most natural, its readiness is because it is most loving, and its reliability is because it is most true. No one could ever perform this service perfectly except Christ alone. We know that our mothers bear us for pain and for death. But what is it that Jesus, our true Mother, does? He who is all-love bears us for joy and eternal life! Blessed may he be! So he sustained us and carried us within himself in love and in labour until the fullness of time, suffering the most agonising pains and the sharpest birth pangs possible, until in the end he died. And when he had finished and given birth to us for bliss, even then his most wonderful love was not satisfied, as he revealed in his high, surpassing words of love: "If I could suffer more I would suffer more."

He could not die any more, but he would not cease working! So he had to feed us, for the most precious love of motherhood has placed upon him this obligation to us. The human mother suckles her child with her own milk, but our most precious Mother, Jesus, feeds us with himself through the Blessed Sacrament, which is the precious food of true life. And through all the sweet Sacraments he sustains us in the greatest mercy and grace. This is what he meant when he said, "It is I whom Holy Church preaches and teaches to you." That is to say, "All the health and life of the Sacraments, all the power and grace of my word, all the goodness set apart for you in Holy Church — it is I."

RDL ch. 60

Now he acts and feeds us
through his sacraments

"Seated at the right hand of the Father" (Mk 14:62; Lk 22:69) and pouring out the Holy Spirit on his Body which is the Church, Christ now acts through the sacraments he instituted to communicate his grace. The sacraments are perceptible signs (words and actions) accessible to our human nature. By the action of Christ and the power of the Holy Spirit they make present efficaciously the grace they signify.

CCC 1084

Come to Mother Jesus
Like a Little Child

Jesus replied:
"I tell you most solemnly,
unless a man is born through water and the Spirit,
he cannot enter the kingdom of God:
what is born of the flesh is flesh;
what is born of the Spirit is spirit.
Do not be surprised when I say:
You must be born from above.
The man who lives by the truth
comes out into the light,
so that it may be plainly seen
that what he does is done in God."

John 3:5-7,21

Prayer: My kind, sweet Jesus, teach me to come to you truly
as a child to its mother.

A mother may sometimes allow her child to fall and be hurt in different ways for its own benefit, but because of her love she could never allow her child to suffer any serious harm. And even if our earthly mother may allow her child to die, our heavenly Mother, Jesus, will never allow us his children to die, for he is almighty, all-wise, and all-love. There is no one like him. Blessed may he be!

But often when our falling and wretchedness is shown to us, we are sorely frightened and so greatly ashamed that we scarcely know where to put ourselves. But then our courteous Mother does not want us to run away, for nothing could be more displeasing to him. No, he wants us to behave like a little child. For the little child, whenever it is distressed or afraid, runs quickly to its mother. And if it can do no more, it calls to the mother for help with all its might. So he wants us to come to him like a weak child and say: "My kind Mother, my gracious Mother, my dear Mother, please forgive me. I'm disgusting — and am not a bit like you. And by myself I am neither able, nor know how, to amend without your help and grace."

Even if we do not immediately feel better let us all the same be sure he is behaving like a wise mother. For if he sees that it is better for us to be sad and tearful, with pity and compassion and out of love for us he allows it until the right time. He wants us to be like a loving child who always naturally trusts its mother's love in good times and bad.

RDL ch. 61

Our mother, born from above, the Body of Christ

The eternal Father, in accordance with the utterly gratuitous and mysterious design of his wisdom and goodness, created the whole universe, and chose to raise up men to share in his own divine life, to which he calls all in his Son.

CCC 759

The Church is the visible plan of God's love for humanity, because God desires that the whole human race may become one People of God, form one Body of Christ, and be built up into one temple of the Holy Spirit.

CCC 776

The Church, further, which is called "that Jerusalem which is above" and "our mother" (Gal 4:26), is described as the spotless spouse of the spotless lamb. It is she whom Christ "loved and for whom he delivered himself up that he might sanctify her". It is she whom he unites to himself by an unbreakable alliance, and whom he constantly "nourishes and cherishes" (cf. Rv 12:17; 19:7; 21:2,9; 22:17; Eph 5:25-26,29).

CCC 757

The Fifteenth Revelation

The Fullness of God's Grace

Before this I had a great longing and desire by the grace of God to be taken out of this world and out of this life.

For I often looked at the misery that is all around here and I thought of the happiness and bliss that is there. Even if there had been no other pain in this life except the absence of our Lord, it would have been more than I could bear, as it seemed to me at times. All this made me mourn and languish with longing. On top of that my own wretchedness, my sloth and weakness made me lose the taste for living and for working as I ought to have done.

To all this our courteous Lord answered, to give me comfort and patience, with these words: "Suddenly you will be taken out of all your pain, all your sickness, all your distress, and all your woe. You shall come up above and you will have me as your reward, and you shall be filled full of joy and bliss."

RDL ch. 64

A Joyful Prospect
and an Immense Comfort

As a doe longs for running streams,
so longs my soul for you, my God.
I have no food but tears day and night;
and all day long men say to me,
"Where is your God?"
Why so downcast, my soul,
why do you sigh within me?
Put your hope in God: I shall praise him yet,
my saviour, my God.
Send out your light and your truth, let these be my guide,
to lead me to your holy mountain
and to the place where you live.
Then I shall go to the altar of God, to the God of my joy,
I shall rejoice, I shall praise you on the harp,
Yahweh, my God.

Psalm 42-43:1, 3, 11, 3, 4

Prayer: Father, by your grace I choose to do your will,
           in thanksgiving and in love of you.

It is much more delightful for us to be taken from pain than for pain to be taken from us; for if pain is taken from us it may return. So for a loving soul this is a tremendous consolation, and most wonderful to know that we shall be taken away from pain. In this promise I saw the merciful compassion that our Lord has for us amid our sorrow, and his courteous promise of complete deliverance, for he wants us to be comforted by this overwhelming joy. He showed this in these words: "You shall come up above and you will have me as your reward, and you shall be filled full of joy and bliss."

It is God's will that we focus on this blessed prospect as often as we can, and with the help of his grace stay with it as long as we can. For to the soul that is led by God this is a most blessed contemplation, and very much to God's honour as long as it lasts.

And when we fall back into ourselves because of depression and spiritual blindness, and through the spiritual and physical pains that we experience because of our frailty, it is God's will that we keep in mind that he has not forgotten us. This is what he means with these words said for our comfort: "You will never again have pain in any form nor any kind of sickness, nor any kind of displeasure or weakness of will, but eternal joy and bliss without end. Why then should it upset you to suffer for me a while, seeing that it is my will and to my glory?"

It is God's will that we should accept his promises and his comfort as generously and as mightily as possible. At the same time he also wants us to bear this waiting and all our troubles as lightly as we can, dismissing them as of no account. For the more lightly we take them and the less value we place on them out of love for him, the less the pain we shall feel when we experience them, and the greater will be our thanks and reward because of them.

RDL ch. 64

Choosing to do what is pleasing to the Father

"Although he was a Son, [Jesus] learned obedience through what he suffered" (Heb 5:8). How much more have we sinful creatures to learn obedience — we who in him have become children of adoption! We ask our Father to unite our will to his Son's, in order to fulfil his will, his plan of salvation for the life of the world. We are radically incapable of this, but united with Jesus and with the power of his Holy

Spirit, we can surrender our will to him and decide to choose what his Son has always chosen: to do what is pleasing to the Father (cf. Jn 8:29).

In committing ourselves to Christ, we can become one spirit with him, and thereby accomplish his will, in such wise that it will be perfect on earth as it is in heaven.

CCC 2825

By prayer we can discern "what is the will of God" and obtain the endurance to do it (Rom 12:2; cf. Eph 5:17; Heb 10:36). Jesus teaches us that one enters heaven not by speaking words, but by doing "the will of my Father in heaven" (Mt 7:21).

CCC 2826

He Has Done All Things for Me, in the Unity of Love

Yahweh, you examine me and know me,
you know if I am standing or sitting,
you read my thoughts from far away,
whether I walk or lie down, you are watching,
you know every detail of my conduct.
It was you who created my inmost self,
and put me together in my mother's womb;
for all these mysteries I thank you:
for the wonder of myself,
for the wonder of your works.

Psalm 139:1-3, 13-14

Prayer: Lord, I thank you and I praise you, for all I have and am is received from you.

It is God's will that I should see myself as duty bound to him in love as if all he had ever done was done for me. And this is how every soul should think about its Lover. That is to say, that the love of God creates such a unity among us that, when it is really seen, no one can separate self from others. So every soul ought to think that God has done for it all that God has ever done.

God reveals this to make us love him, delight him, and to teach us to fear nothing but him. It is his will that we should know that all the power of our enemy is the hands of our Friend. Therefore the soul who is sure of this will fear nothing except the One who is loved, and will relegate every other fear to a place among the emotions, physical sickness and imagined fantasies. So, even though we may be in such great pain, woe and distress that it seems we can think of nothing else but the state in which we find ourselves, as soon as we can we try to shrug it off and dismiss it as nothing. Why? Because God wants us to know him; and if we know him, love him, and reverently fear him, we shall have patience and be in great rest. Then all that God does will bring us great pleasure. This was shown in our Lord's words: "Why then should it upset you to suffer for a while, seeing it is my will and to my glory?"

RDL ch. 65

Our feelings are not a reliable measure

Since it belongs to the supernatural order, grace *escapes our experience* and cannot be known except by faith. We cannot therefore rely on our feelings or our works to conclude that we are justified and saved. However, according to the Lord's words — "Thus you will know them by their fruits" (Mt 7:20) — reflection on God's blessings in our life and in the lives of the saints offers us a guarantee that grace is at work in us and spurs us on to an ever greater faith and an attitude of trustful poverty.

A pleasing illustration of this attitude is found in the reply of St. Joan of Arc to a question posed as a trap by her ecclesiastical judges: "Asked if she knew that she was in God's grace, she replied: 'If I am not, may it please God to put me in it; if I am, may it please God to keep me there.' "

CCC 2005

The Sixteenth Revelation

Life Everlasting

Then the Lord opened my siritual eyes and showed me my soul in the middle of my heart.

I saw the soul was as large as if it were an endless citadel and a blessed kingdom. From the conditions that I saw in it, I could tell that it is a glorious city. In the midst of that city sits our Lord Jesus, true God and true Man, a handsome person and of tall stature, highest bishop, most majestic king, and most glorious Lord. I saw him arrayed with great majesty and honour. He sits in the soul in unchanging peace and in rest, and he rules and sustains heaven and earth and all that exists. The Divinity rules and governs without any instrument or effort; the soul is totally immersed in the blessed Godhead, who is supreme power, supreme wisdom and supreme goodness.

The place that Jesus takes in our soul, he will never ever leave again, as I see it, for in us is his homeliest home and his eternal dwelling.

RDL ch. 67

You Will Not Be Overcome

Then I remembered your mercy, Lord,
and your deeds from earliest times,
how you deliver those who wait for you patiently,
and save them from the clutches of their enemies.
And I sent up my plea from the earth,
I begged to be delivered from death,
I called on the Lord, the father of my Lord,
"Do not desert me in the days of ordeal,
in the time of my helplessness against the proud."
And my plea was heard, for you saved me from destruction,
you delivered me from that time of evil.
Ecclesiasticus 51:8-10a, 11

Prayer: Lord, I do feel apprehension; help me believe
that in you I shall not be overcome.

Our Lord confirmed to me that he was the one who had revealed everything to me. When I had contemplated this with diligence, our good Lord revealed to me most sweetly some words, without voice and without opening his lips, just as he had done before; he said: "Be now quite certain that what you saw today was not a delusion; but accept it, believe it, and firmly hold on to it, be comforted by it and trust in it, and you shall not be overcome."

All this teaching and true comfort is meant for all my fellow-Christians, as I have already said, and this is the will of God.

And these words: "You shall not be overcome," were said very insistently and very powerfully in order to give me certainty and comfort against every tribulation that may come my way. He did not say: "You shall not be tempted; you shall not be burdened; you shall not be distressed," but he said: "You shall not be overcome." God wants us to pay attention to these words and to be mighty in faithful trust, in good and in bad times. God loves us and delights in us, so he wishes us to love and delight in him and greatly trust him. Thus all will be well.

RDL ch.68

God cares for all, from the least to the greatest

The witness of Scripture is unanimous that the solicitude of divine providence is *concrete* and *immediate*; God cares for all, from the least things to the great events of the world and its history. The sacred books powerfully affirm God's absolute sovereignty over the course of events: "Our God is in the heavens; he does whatever he pleases" (Ps 115:3). And so it is with Christ, "who opens and no one shall shut, who shuts and no one opens" (Rv 3:7). As the book of Proverbs states: "Many are the plans in the mind of a man, but it is the purpose of the Lord that will be established" (Prv 19:21).

CCC 303

Christ invites us to filial trust in the providence of our heavenly Father (cf. Mt 6:26-34), and Peter the apostle repeats: "Cast all your anxieties on him, for he cares about you" (1 Pt 5:7; cf. Ps 55:23).

CCC 322

Stay within Faith

Cling to him and do not leave him,
so that you may be honoured at the end of your days.
Whatever happens to you, accept it,
and in the uncertainties of your humble state, be patient,
since gold is tested in the fire,
and chosen men in the furnace of humiliation.
Trust him and he will uphold you,
follow a straight path and hope in him.
For the Lord is compassionate and merciful,
he forgives sins, and saves in days of distress.
Let us fall into the hands of the Lord,
not into the hands of men;
for as his majesty is,
so too is his mercy.

Ecclesiasticus 2:3-6, 11, 18

Prayer: My Jesus, that I may truly accept your teaching,
and follow it faithfully and joyfully.

His intention when he gave me these words, beginning, "Accept it," was to teach us to hold it fast in our heart, for he wants it to abide with us in faith to the end of our life, and afterwards be with us in complete joy. He wants us always faithfully to trust in his blessed promises through knowing his goodness.

For our faith is opposed in many ways within and without by our own blindness and by our spiritual enemies. Therefore our precious Lover helps us with spiritual insight and true teaching in various ways, both inwardly and outwardly, so that we may know him. However, whatever way he teaches us, he wants us to apprehend him wisely, receive him sweetly, and to keep ourselves firmly in him. For beyond faith there is no goodness available in this life, as I see it, and below faith there is no health of soul. It is *within* faith that our Lord wants us to stay. For it is his goodness and his working which keeps us in the faith; and it is by his permission that our spiritual enemy tests our faith, thus making us stronger. For if our faith had no opposition it would deserve no reward. That is how I understand our Lord's meaning.

RDL ch.70

Living faith works through love

Faith is the theological virtue by which we believe in God and believe all that he has said and revealed to us, and that Holy Church proposes for our belief, because he is truth itself. By faith man freely commits his entire self to God. For this reason the believer seeks to know and do God's will. "The righteous shall live by faith." Living faith "work[s] through charity" (Rom1:17; Gal 5:6).

CCC 1814

The disciple of Christ must not only keep the faith and live on it, but also profess it, confidently bear witness to it and spread it: all however must be prepared to confess Christ before men and to follow him along the way of the Cross, amidst the persecutions which the Church never lacks. Service of and witness to the faith are necessary for salvation: "so every one who acknowledges me before men, I also will acknowledge before my Father who is in heaven; but whoever denies me before men, I also will deny before my Father who is in heaven" (Mt 10:32-33)

CCC 1816

He Is always Looking at Us

I lift my eyes to you,
to you who have your home in heaven,
eyes like the eyes of slaves
fixed on their master's hand;
like the eyes of a slave-girl
fixed on the hand of her mistress,
so our eyes are fixed on Yahweh our God,
for him to take pity on us.

Psalm 123:1-2

Prayer: Jesus, by your grace, make my conduct conform
more and more to my inner disposition.

G lad and joyful and sweet is the blessed and lovely expression our Lord shows to our souls; for he sees us always
living in love-longing, and he wants our souls to turn gladly to
him to give him his reward. And so I hope that, through his
grace, he will continue to make our outward conduct conform
more and more to our inner disposition and make us all one
with him and with each other in that true lasting joy which is
Jesus.

I see in our Lord's face three kinds of expression. When we
are in pain and distress he reveals to us the face of his Passion
and his Cross, helping us to bear ours with his own blessed
power. And although this sight is mournful and sorrowful, yet
it remains glad and joyful because he is God. When we sin he
shows us the expression of pity and compassion, powerfully
protecting us against all our enemies. These are the two usual
expressions which he shows to us in this life. Mixed with
them is the third; namely, that blessed face, partially as it will
be in heaven without end. This comes through his touch of
grace in the sweet light of the Spirit, through which we are

kept in true faith, hope and love, in repentance and in devotion, as well as in contemplation and all the experiences of true refreshment and sweet consolation.

RDL ch.71

After baptismal conversion, a second conversion is called for from all

Peter's conversion after he had denied his master three times bears witness to this. Jesus' look of infinite mercy drew tears of repentance from Peter and, after the Lord's Resurrection, a threefold affirmation of love for him (cf. Lk 22:61; Jn 21:15-17). The second conversion also has a *communitarian* dimension, as is clear in the Lord's call to a whole Church: "Repent!" (Rv 2:5, 16). Ambrose says of the two conversions that, in the Church, "there are water and tears: the water of Baptism and the tears of repentance."

CCC 1429

The movement of return to God, called conversion and repentance, entails sorrow for and abhorrence of sins committed, and the firm purpose of sinning no more in the future. Conversion touches the past and the future, and is nourished by hope of God's mercy.

CCC 1490

He Forgets — We Ourselves
Must also Forget

Come, you must set your heart right,
stretch out your hands to him.
Renounce the iniquity which stains your hands,
let no injustice live within your tents.
Then you may face the world in innocence,
unwavering and free from fear.
You will forget your sufferings,
remember them as waters that have passed away.
Your life, more radiant than the noonday,
will make a dawn of darkness.
Full of hope, you will live secure,
dwelling well and safely guarded.

Job 11:13-18

Prayer: Lord, help me put aside what has been, in renewal
and your promise of what is to come.

When we start to hate sin, and amend our ways
according to the laws of Holy Church, there still
persists a fear which hinders us. This is because we remain
looking at ourselves and at the sins we have committed in the
past; sins which may have been deadly. Then, because we do
not keep our promises or are unable to keep the purity in
which our Lord has placed us, we often fall back into great
wretchedness and shame. When we see all this we are so sorry
and depressed that we can hardly find any comfort.

Sometimes we take this fear as being humility, but it is a
shameful blindness and a weakness. We do not despise it as
we do any other sin, because we do not recognise it. In fact it

comes from lack of true judgement, for it comes from the enemy and it is contrary to truth.[1]

Of all the attributes of the Blessed Trinity, it is God's will that we have most confidence, delight and encouragement in his love. For it is love which makes strength and wisdom accessible to us. For just as God in his kindness forgets our sin as soon as we repent, so likewise he wishes us to forget our sin, especially as far as our unreasonable depression and our doubting fear is concerned.

Doubting fear leads us to despair, but God wants to transform fear into love by giving us true knowledge of love; that is to say, he wants the bitterness of doubt to be turned into the sweetness of gentle love. For it never pleases our Lord when his servants doubt his goodness.

RDL ch. 73; ch. 74

Cling to hope in confident expectation, never to despair

When God reveals himself and calls him, man cannot fully respond to the divine love by his own powers. He must hope that God will give him the capacity to love

---

1. When the penitent person becomes conscious of his sinfulness, the father of lies tries to deceive him or her into a false, fear-filled "humility" in which the sinner cringes from God because he or she feels so totally unworthy. But this self-judgement and lack of trust blocks the path of return to God; for God never forces but tenderly invites us — and he never judges those who do not judge (Lk 6:37). We are not even to judge our own selves (1 Cor 4:3). So this unholy fear and misleading, false humility should be firmly rejected. Julian has already taught us that in the end God will, through the power of Christ's passion, generate a greater good from our sin and make everything well that is not well. So we should not dwell on our evil and sorrow nor grieve over it. God "wants us to be less anxious and more at peace in love, and to stop looking at all the worrying things that hold us back from truly enjoying him" (RDL ch. 32).

him in return and to act in conformity with the commandments of charity. Hope is the confident expectation of divine blessing and the beatific vision of God; it is also the fear of offending God's love and of incurring punishment.

CCC 2090

By *despair*, man ceases to hope for his personal salvation from God, for help in attaining it or for the forgiveness of his sins. Despair is contrary to God's goodness, to his justice — for the Lord is faithful to his promises — and to his mercy.

CCC 2091

The Tender Fear
That Is Reverential Awe

Do not be afraid, for I have redeemed you;
I have called you by your name, you are mine.
Should you pass through the sea, I will be with you;
or through rivers, they will not swallow you up.
Should you walk through fire, you will not be scorched
and the flames will not burn you.
For I am Yahweh, your God,
the Holy One of Israel, your saviour.
Do not be afraid, for I am with you.

Isaiah 43:1b-3, 5a

Prayer: Lord, the fear I want is wonder-struck reverence, as when I look into the starry depths.

Reverent fear is the only fear that really pleases God. It is the most tender of fears, for the more of this gentle fear one has the less is it actually felt, in the sweetness of his utter love.

Love and fear are brothers, and their roots have been planted in us by the goodness of our Creator, and they shall never be taken from us. It is in our nature to love, and by grace we love. Likewise, it is in our nature to fear, but we are also given grace to fear. It belongs to God's Lordship and Fatherhood to be feared, as it belongs to his goodness to be loved. And it belongs to us, his servants and children, to fear him for his Lordship and Fatherhood, as it belongs to us to love him for his Goodness.

Every other fear that presents itself to us which is not reverent fear, even if it comes under the guise of holiness, is not quite true. This is how they can be recognised apart. The fear that makes us turn quickly away from everything that is not good, and with all our heart and mind fall into our Lord's breast, as a child into its mother's arms, knowing our weakness and great need, knowing his everlasting goodness and blessed love, seeking only his salvation, clinging to him with faithful trust — the fear that makes us do all that is gentle and gracious, good and true, and comes from God's grace and is natural, good and true.

Any fear that does not lead us to do this is either wrong or tainted. So the remedy for this is therefore to recognise both kinds of fear and refuse the wrong one.

RDL ch. 74

Responding to God's call to his graced children

Our justification comes from the grace of God. Grace is *favour*, the *free and undeserved help* that God gives us to respond to his call to become children of God, adoptive

sons, partakers of the divine nature and of eternal life
(cf. Jn 1:12-18; 17:3; Rom 8:14-17; 2 Pt 1:3-4).

CCC 1996

Grace is a participation in the life of God. It introduces
us into the intimacy of Trinitarian life: by Baptism the
Christian participates in the grace of Christ, the Head
of his Body. As an "adopted son" he can henceforth
call God "Father," in union with the only Son. He
receives the life of the Spirit who breathes charity into
him and who forms the Church.

CCC 1997

Whether Filthy or Clean,
Cling to Jesus

The angel of Yahweh said to Satan,
"May Yahweh rebuke you, Satan, may Yahweh rebuke you,
he who has made Jerusalem his very own.
Is not this man a brand snatched from the fire?"
Now Joshua was dressed in dirty clothes
as he stood before the angel of Yahweh.
The angel said these words to those who stood before him,
"Take off his dirty clothes and clothe him
in splendid robes of state, and put a clean turban on his head."
They clothed him in splendid robes of state
and put a clean turban on his head.
The angel of Yahweh was standing there and said to him,
"Look, I have taken away your iniquity from you."

Zechariah 3:2-5

Prayer: Lord, I often feel filthy and unfit; wash, clothe
and heal me, that I may joy in you.

In this blessed revelation of our Lord I understand two opposite things. One is the wisest thing any creature can do in this life; the other is the most stupid thing. The wisest thing is to behave according to the will and counsel of our greatest, royal Friend. This blessed Friend is Jesus, and his will and counsel is that we cling to him and hold tightly to him always, no matter what state we may be in. Whether we are filthy or clean, we are always the same to him in his love. Whether for good or for bad, he never wants us to run away from him. It is because of our own fickleness that we so often fall into sin and then, in our stupidity and blindness and at the prompting of the enemy, we get this doubting fear.

It says: "You know well that you are a wretch, a sinner and unfaithful because you do not keep your covenant. Often you promise the Lord you will do better, then in no time at all you fall back into the same sin, especially into sloth and time-wasting!" Here lies the beginning of sin, as I see it, especially for those creatures in the service of the Lord by inward contemplation of his blessed goodness. All of this makes us afraid to come before our courteous Lord.

In this way our enemy seeks to set us back by filling us full of false fears about our wretchedness, and the pain with which he oppresses us. He wants to depress us and wear us out to such an extent that we quite forget the blissful contemplation of our eternal Friend, Jesus.

RDL ch. 76

The depths of his love, the abyss of his mercy

The process of conversion and repentance was described by Jesus in the parable of the prodigal son, the centre of which is the merciful father (cf. Lk 15:11-24): the fascination of illusory freedom, the abandonment of the father's house; the extreme misery in which the son finds himself after squandering his fortune; his deep humiliation at finding himself obliged to feed swine, and still worse, at wanting to feed on the husks the pigs ate; his reflection on all he has lost; his repentance and decision to declare himself guilty before his father; the journey back; the father's generous welcome; the father's joy — all these are characteristic of the process of conversion. The beautiful robe, the ring and the festive banquet are symbols of that new life — pure, worthy and joyful — of anyone who returns to God and to the bosom of his family, which is the Church. Only the heart of Christ who knows the depths of his Father's love could reveal to us the abyss of his mercy in so simple and beautiful a way.

CCC 1439

Rejoice in the Remedy He Gives Us

I am taking action here and now
against your oppressors.
When that time comes I will rescue the lame,
and gather the strays,
and I will win them praise and renown
when I restore their fortunes.
When that time comes I will be your guide,
when that time comes, I will gather you in;
I will give you praise and renown
among all the peoples on earth
when I restore your fortunes under your own eyes,
says Yahweh.

Zephaniah 3:19-20

Prayer: Lord of hope and happiness, in you I trust, I cling, I shelter; for you I live and work.

This world is a prison and this life is a penance. However, God wants us to rejoice in the remedy for it. The remedy is that our Lord is with us, protecting us and leading us into the fullness of joy. Our Lord intends this to be an endless joy for us; that he who will be our bliss when we are up there, is now, whilst we are down here, our protector, our way and our heaven in true love and faithful trust. This he gave me to understand in all the revelations, especially when he showed me his Passion, and he made me fervently choose him to be my heaven.

Let us flee to our Lord and we shall be comforted. Let us touch him and we shall be made clean. Let us cleave to him and we shall be safe and secure from every kind of harm. Our courteous Lord wants us to feel as at home with him as the heart can conceive or the soul desire. But let us be careful not to treat this close friendship so casually that we forget courtesy. For while our Lord is utter homeliness, he is as courteous as he is homely, for he is true courtesy. And he wants his blessed ones, who will be in heaven with him for ever, to be like him in all things; for to be exactly like our Lord is our true salvation and our utter bliss. If we do not know how we shall do all this, then let us request it from our Lord, and he will teach us, for it is his delight and his glory — blessed be he!

RDL ch. 77

Led to the happiness that flows from love

Hope is the theological virtue by which we desire the Kingdom of heaven and eternal life as our happiness, placing our trust in Christ's promises and relying not on our own strength, but on the help of the grace of the Holy Spirit. "Let us hold fast the confession of our hope without wavering, for he who promised is faithful"(Heb 10:23). "The Holy Spirit . . . he poured out upon us richly through Jesus Christ our Saviour, so that we might be justified by his grace and become heirs in hope of eternal life" (Ti 3:6-7).

CCC 1817

The virtue of hope responds to the aspiration to happiness which God has placed in the heart of every man; it takes up the hopes that inspire men's activities and purifies them so as to order them to the Kingdom of heaven; it keeps man from discouragement; it sustains him during times of abandonment; it opens up his heart in expectation of eternal beatitude. Buoyed up by hope, he is preserved from selfishness and led to the happiness that flows from charity.

CCC 1818

We Are His Joy and Delight

Yahweh is my light and my salvation,
whom need I fear?
Yahweh is the fortress of my life,
of whom should I be afraid?
Though an army pitched camp against me,
my heart would not fear;
though war were waged against me,
my trust would still be firm.
This I believe: I shall see the goodness of Yahweh,
in the land of the living.
Put your hope in Yahweh, be strong,
let your heart be bold, put your hope in Yahweh.

Psalm 27:1, 3, 13-14

Prayer: My Joy and Delight, enfold me in your love, that I may bring it to others.

Our courteous Lord also showed me most powerfully that his love never ends and never changes and that, because of his great goodness and his safe keeping of us by his grace, our souls shall never ever be separated from his love.

This friendly revelation from our kind Lord is a lovely lesson, a sweet and gracious message from himself to comfort our soul. He wants us to know through the sweetness and homeliness of his love that all that we see and feel, both within and without, which is in opposition to this, is from the enemy and not from God. For example, if we are moved to be more careless in our way of living or in the custody of our heart because we have had such an experience of God's rich love, then we must be very much on our guard. If such an impulse comes, it is false, and we ought to greatly hate it, because it bears no resemblance to God's will.

When we have fallen through frailty or blindness, then our courteous Lord raises us up with his gentle touch and protects us. He wants us to see how wretched we are and humbly face up to it. But he does not want us to stay like that, or to be preoccupied with self-accusations or to wallow in self-pity. But he wants us quickly to turn to him, for he stands all alone, and always waits for us, sorrowing and grieving until we come. He hurries to bring us back to himself, for we are his joy and his delight, and he is our salvation and our life.

RDL ch. 79

The turning again of the heart, then the fruits of conversion

Jesus' call to conversion and penance, like that of the prophets before him, does not aim first at outward works, "sackcloth and ashes," fasting and mortification, but at the *conversion of the heart, interior conversion.* Without this, such penances remain sterile and false; however, interior conversion urges expression in visible signs, gestures and works of penance (cf. Jl 2:12-13; Is 1:16-17; Mt 6:1-6, 16-18).

CCC 1430

Conversion is accomplished in daily life by gestures of reconciliation, concern for the poor, the exercise and defence of justice and right (cf. Am 5:24; Is 1:17), by the admission of faults to one's brethren, fraternal correction, revision of life, examination of conscience, spiritual direction, acceptance of suffering, endurance of persecution for the sake of righteousness. Taking up one's cross each day and following Jesus is the surest way of penance (cf. Lk 9:23).

CCC 1435

Helped, Protected, Saved

Happy the man who meditates on wisdom,
and reasons with good sense,
who studies her ways in his heart,
and ponders her secrets.
He pursues her like a hunter,
and lies in wait by her path;
he peeps in at her windows,
and listens at her doors;
he lodges close to her house,
and fixes his peg in her walls;
he pitches his tent at her side,
and lodges in an excellent lodging;
he sets his children in her shade,
and camps beneath her branches,
he is sheltered by her from the heat,
and in her glory he makes his home.

Ecclesiasticus 14:20-27

Prayer: Grace-giving Spirit, I praise you for your gifts to me;
make them fruitful for others.

We are supported in this life by three things; with these three things God is worshipped and we are helped, protected and saved.

The first is the use of our natural reason; the second is the everyday teaching of Holy Church; the third is the inner grace-giving work of the Holy Spirit. And these three are from the one God. God is the ground of our natural reason; God is the teaching of Holy Church; God is the Holy Spirit. All are different gifts which he wants us to value highly and pay attention to. Together these gifts are continually at work in us and do great things. He wants us to know about the greatness of these things while here on earth, like learning the alphabet. This means that we can know some elementary knowledge here to help us on our way; of that knowledge we shall have fullness in heaven.

RDL ch. 80

The gifts of the light of reason, the sense of faith

The human person participates in the light and power of the divine Spirit. By his reason, he is capable of understanding the order of things established by the Creator. By free will, he is capable of directing himself toward his true good. He finds his perfection in seeking and loving what is true and good.

CCC 1704

In order to preserve the Church in the purity of the faith handed on by the apostles, Christ who is the Truth willed to confer on her a share in his infallibility. By a supernatural sense of faith the People of God, under the guidance of the Church's living Magisterium, unfailingly adheres to this faith.

CCC 889

Living Gladly and Joyfully

I want you to be happy, always happy in the Lord;
I repeat, what I want is your happiness.
Let your tolerance be evident to everyone:
the Lord is very near.
There is no need to worry;
but if there is anything you need, pray for it,
asking God for it with prayer and thanksgiving,
and that peace of God,
which is so much greater than we can understand,
will guard your hearts and your thoughts,
in Christ Jesus.

Philippians 4:4-7

Prayer: Father, I accept my pains for the sake of the joy which even now comes to me.

Out of all the things we can do in our penance for our sin, the one which gives God most honour is to live gladly and joyfully for love of him. For he looks at us so tenderly that he sees our whole life here as a penance. All our nature longs for him, and this is a lasting penance for us. It is he himself who produces it, and mercifully helps us to bear it. His love makes him long for us; his wisdom and truth and justice make him wait for us while we are here; and he wants to see this longing and waiting in us. This is our natural penance and the highest, as it seems to me, because this penance will never leave us until we are completely fulfilled, when we shall love God as our reward. Therefore he wants us to set our hearts on our "passing-over" — that is, our passing from the pain we feel now, into the bliss that we trust in.

RDL ch. 81

The desire for happiness

The Beatitudes (cf. Mt 5:3-12) respond to the natural desire for happiness. This desire is of divine origin: God has placed it in the human heart in order to draw man to the One who alone can fulfil it: "We all want to live happily; in the whole human race there is no one who does not assent to this proposition, even before it is fully articulated. How is it, then, that I seek you, Lord? Since in seeking you, my God, I seek a happy life, let me seek you so that my soul may live, for my body draws life from my soul and my soul draws life from you."[2] God alone satisfies.

CCC 1718

The New Testament uses several expressions to characterise the beatitude to which God calls man:
- the coming of the Kingdom of God (cf. Mt 4:17);
- the vision of God: "Blessed are the pure in heart, for they shall see God" (Mt 5:8; cf. 1 Jn 3:2; 1 Cor 13:12);
- entering into the joy of the Lord (Mt 25:21-23);
- entering into God's rest (cf. Heb 4:7-11).

CCC 1720

2. Augustine of Hippo, *Confessions* X:20.

The Light of Love

Set me like a seal on your heart,
like a seal on your arm.
For love is strong as Death,
jealousy relentless as Sheol.
The flash of it is like a flash of fire,
a flame of Yahweh himself.
Love no flood can quench,
no torrents drown.

Song of Songs 8:6-7

Prayer:　My precious Light and dearest Love, make me
a river of your love to others.

The light is love, which God in his wisdom measures out to us in a way which is beautiful and which is best for us. The light is not bright enough to enable us to see now our most Blessed Day, but neither is that day totally obscured. It is enough light by which we can live a rewarding life of hard work, discerning the glorious thanks of God. This I saw in the sixth Revelation, where he said: "I thank you for your service and your labour." So love keeps us in faith and hope; and faith and hope lead us in love. And in the end all will be love.

This light of love I understood in three ways. The first is un-created love; the second is created love; the third is given love. Uncreated love is God; created love is our soul in God; given love is virtue. Given love is a precious gift of grace which God works in us, through which we love God for himself, and ourselves in God; and we love all that God loves, for the sake of God.

RDL ch. 84

Faith and hope lead us to love

We can therefore hope in the glory of heaven promised
by God to those who love him and do his will (cf. Rom
8:28-30; Mt 7:21). In every circumstance, each one of
us should hope, with the grace of God, to persevere to
"the end" (Mt 10:22) and to obtain the joy of heaven,
as God's eternal reward for the good works accomplished with the grace of Christ. In hope, the Church
prays for "all men to be saved" (1 Tm 2:4). She longs to
be united with Christ, her Bridegroom, in the glory of
heaven: "Hope, O my soul, hope. You know neither
the day nor the hour. Watch carefully, for everything
passes quickly, even though your impatience makes
doubtful what is certain, and turns a very short time
into a long one. Dream that the more you struggle, the
more you prove the love that you bear your God, and
the more you will rejoice one day with your Beloved, in
a happiness and rapture that can never end."[3]

CCC 1821

---

3. Teresa of Avila, *Exclamaciones del alma a Dios* 15:3.

We Praise You, Lord, All Is Well

Yahweh, you are my God,
I extol you, I praise your name;
for you have carried out your excellent design,
long planned, trustworthy, true.
On this mountain he will remove
the mourning veil covering all peoples,
and the shroud enwrapping all nations,
he will destroy Death for ever.
The Lord Yahweh will wipe away
the tears from every cheek;
he will take away his people's shame
everywhere on earth,
for Yahweh has said so.
We exult and we rejoice that he has saved us.

Isaiah 25:1, 7-8, 9b

Prayer:	Lord, I praise you because it is like this;
	I know all will be well.

As truly as we shall be in the bliss of God without end, praising and thanking him, so truly have we been in the foresight of God, loved and known by him as part of his eternal plan from without beginning. In his timeless love he made us, and in this same love he protects us, and never allows us to be hurt in any way which would diminish our eternal bliss.

When the Judgement is announced and we are all brought up above, then we shall clearly see in God the mysteries which are now hidden from us. Then none of us will have the slightest urge to say, "Lord, if it had been like this, then it would have been fine." Instead we shall all say with one voice; "Lord, blessed may you be, because it is like this: all is well. Now we can truly see that everything has been done just as you planned it before anything was made."

RDL ch. 85

Journeying toward perfection

God is the sovereign master of his plan. But to carry it out he also makes use of his creatures' co-operation. This use is not a sign of weakness, but rather a token of almighty God's greatness and goodness. For God grants his creatures not only their existence, but also the dignity of acting on their own, of being causes and principles for each other, and thus of co-operating in the accomplishment of his plan.

CCC 306

With infinite power God could always create something better. But with infinite wisdom and goodness God freely willed to create a world in a state of journeying towards its ultimate perfection.

CCC 310

All This We Shall See in God, for Evermore

Love is always patient and kind;
it is never jealous; love is never boastful or conceited;
it is never rude or selfish;
it does not take offence, and is not resentful.
Love takes no pleasure in other people's sins
but delights in the truth;
it is always ready to excuse, to trust, to hope,
and to endure whatever comes.
In short, there are three things that last;
faith, hope and love;
and the greatest of these is love.

1 Corinthians 13:4-7, 13

Prayer: My God and Love, in my journey to you I trust you,
I thank you, I joy in you.

In love, let us all join together in prayer, in union with God working in us; thanking, trusting, rejoicing, and enjoying him. That is how our good Lord wants us to pray to him, as far as I can see from his intention in everything he said, and especially from his sweet words which were spoken so cheerfully: "I am the ground of your beseeching."

For truly I saw and understood our Lord to mean that he revealed it all because he wants it to be better known than it is. And as we come to know it he will give us grace to love him and cling to him. He looks at his heavenly treasure on earth with such great love that he will give us more light and comfort in the joy of heaven, thus drawing our hearts to him, away from the sorrow and gloom in which we now are.

I was given a spiritual understanding, and I was told: "Do you want to know what our Lord meant in all this? Know it well: love was his meaning. Who showed it to you? Love. What did he show you? Love. Why did he show it to you? For love. Remain firm in this love and you will taste of it ever more deeply; but you will never know anything else from it, for ever and ever."

So I was taught that love was what our Lord meant. And I saw with absolute certainty that before God made us he loved us, and that his love never slackened, nor ever will. In this love he has done all his works, in this love he has made all things for our benefit, and in this love our life is everlasting. In our creation we had a beginning, but the love in which he created us was in him for ever and never had a beginning. In this love we have our beginning.

And all this we shall see in God, without end. Thanks be to God!

RDL ch. 86

The fruit and goal of our journey

Charity is the theological virtue by which we love God above all things for his own sake, and our neighbour as ourselves for the love of God.

CCC 1822

Christ died out of love for us, while we were still "enemies" (Rom 5:10). The Lord asks us to love as he does, even our *enemies*, to make ourselves the neighbour of those furthest away, and to love children and the poor as Christ himself (cf. Mt 5:44; Lk 10:27-37; Mk 9:37; Mt 25:40, 45).

CCC 1825

The *fruits* of charity are joy, peace and mercy; charity demands beneficence and fraternal correction; it is benevolence; it fosters reciprocity and remains disinterested and generous; it is friendship and communion: Love itself is the fulfilment of all our works. There is the goal; that is why we run; we run toward it, and once we reach it, in it we shall find rest.

CCC 1829

Acknowledgements

The extracts from scripture are from *The Jerusalem Bible*, published and copyright © 1966, 1967 and 1968 by Darton, Longman and Todd, Ltd., London, and Doubleday & Co. Inc., New York, and are used by kind permission of the publishers.

The extracts from the *Catechism of the Catholic Church* are from the English translation published 1994 by Geoffrey Chapman, a Cassell imprint, London, and copyright © 1994 Geoffrey Chapman-Libreria Editrice Vaticana, and are used by kind permission of The Continuum International Publishing Company Group Ltd., London, on behalf of the publishers.

The extracts from the translation by Josef Pischler of the *Revelations of Divine Love by Mother Julian of Norwich* are used by kind permission of the copyright holder, Sr. Elizabeth Ruth Obbard, O.Carm.